50

Teach® Yourself

50 ways to improve your French

Marie-Jo Morelle and
Lorna Wright

If

business, computing and education.

British Library Cataloguing in Publication Data: a catalogue record for this title is available from the British Library.

Library of Congress Catalog Card Number: on file.

First published in UK 2010 by Hodder Education, part of Hachette UK, 338 Euston Road, London NW1 3BH.

First published in US 2010 by The McGraw-Hill Companies, Inc.

This edition published 2010.

The Teach Yourself name is a registered trade mark of Hachette UK.

Typeset by MPS Limited, A Macmillan Company.

Printed in Great Britain for Hodder Education, an Hachette UK Company, 338 Euston Road, London NW1 3BH.

The publisher has used its best endeavours to ensure that the URLs for external websites referred to in this book are correct and active at the time of going to press. However, the publisher and the author have no responsibility for the websites and can make no guarantee that a site will remain live or that the content will remain relevant, decent or appropriate.

Hachette UK's policy is to use papers that are natural, renewable and recyclable products and made from wood grown in sustainable forests. The logging and manufacturing processes are expected to conform to the environmental regulations of the country of origin.

Impression number	10 9 8 7 6 5 4 3 2 1
Year	2014 2013 2012 2011 2010

Dedication and acknowledgements

To all the students who, over many years, have provided us with material for this book and to Daisy, Lorna's youngest ever pupil who, aged one, has never made any of these mistakes!

We should like to thank Geraldine, Andrew and Richard Hutchison and Ben Wright whose support and technical skills have made the production of this book so much easier.

Credits

Front cover: Oxford Illustrators Ltd

Back cover: © Jakub Semeniuk/iStockphoto.com, © Royalty-Free/Corbis, © agencyby/iStockphoto.com, © Andy Cook/iStockphoto.com, © Christopher Ewing/iStockphoto.com, © zebicho – Fotolia.com, © Geoffrey Holman/iStockphoto.com, © Photodisc/Getty Images, © James C. Pruitt/iStockphoto.com, © Mohamed Saber – Fotolia.com

Contents

Nouns, adjectives and adverbs

Verbs: what you do, and when

Prepositions

Weeding out unnecessary words and adding others

Meet the authors

Marie-Jo Morelle

Born and educated in France, I arrived in England in my twenties. As the eldest of five siblings, I always had an interest in making learning a stimulating and fun experience. In the early years, I wanted to bring my family and friends to whatever level of competence I had reached and then, later in my teaching, to make language an instant and useful tool of communication. My father encouraged me to study law and I had a passion for philosophy and psychology: I happily merged all of this into teaching. Constantly re-evaluating language, its role and meaning in society, I adapt my teaching methods to make them more effective in a changing world. My interest in cultural differences was born from my efforts to understand why and how ideologies change in any society. Teaching and researching have helped me value communication above grammar, restoring communication to its original purpose.

Lorna Wright

'Definitely not a teacher' was what I trotted out to anyone who wanted to know what I was going to do when I grew up. It just didn't sound exciting enough, and had a dull, predictable quality about it which didn't appeal in the least. But, by a circuitous route, it is what I have discovered I love doing, and exciting is what it has turned out to be.

My first job in a nursery school in Bordeaux, inventing action games in English for lively toddlers, was the first step in understanding that having fun is a key element in the learning process. This is just as true for the adults I teach today as it was for those young learners in the past, albeit through an involvement which is more cerebral and less physical! I hope that the light-hearted approach of this book will help you, the reader, to speak better French and enjoy it.

Only got a minute?

The French language

French language and culture are recognized worldwide. French is currently spoken by about 80 million people as a first language, by 190 million as a second language, and by another 200 million people as an acquired foreign language.

A lot of its vocabulary is recognizable by English speakers, whose language shares a similar history. As a descendant of the Latin language of the Roman Empire, the development of the French language was also influenced by the native Celtic languages of Roman Gaul and by the Germanic languages. An early form of the French language was brought to England by the Normans after the conquest of England in 1066.

English and French share a growing common vocabulary, e.g. **le club**, **le hamburger**, **dispatcher** and **le planning** (*a schedule*). But such similarities can lead to problems since French pronunciation and ways of putting sentences together follow patterns particular, some may say peculiar, to French. There are, however, significant differences, e.g. nouns in French are grouped into two major categories – masculine (**un**) and feminine (**une**), and word endings, which in French are not always pronounced. The list of potential pitfalls is long and needs to be addressed in the early stages of learning.

This is not a standard grammar book which tells you everything about the workings of the language. It focuses instead on the recurrent challenges with which you as a beginner, intermediate or even quite advanced student are faced. We have exposed 50 common mistakes, shown you the funny side of some of them, and have explained in simple terms why they are incorrect and how to put them right.

5 Only got five minutes?

The French language

French is spoken by over 400 million people across the world.

As a descendant of the Latin language of the Roman Empire, the development of the French language was also influenced by the native Celtic languages of Roman Gaul and by the Germanic languages of the post-Roman Frankish invaders. This explains why so many words are recognizable by English speakers whose language shares a similar history, although the Latin influence is stronger in French. With social usage, some words originating from the Latin language have followed differing paths and their original meanings have changed. Apparently similar words can have divergent meanings, e.g. **biologique**, which can mean either *biological* or *organic*.

Within Europe, French used to be the language spoken by the elite. On today's world stage, thanks to Monsieur de Coubertin, considered the instigator of the Modern Olympic Movement, it has retained some of its status as one of the official languages for the Olympics and, together with English, it is still used in all NATO communications.

The French language is also evident in artistic discourse: literature, philosophy, painting, architecture, dance, theatre, fashion and cinema. Cookery books are full of French expressions and the world still values the high quality of some French wines. French is also a language which has inspired ideas, emotions and revolutions, and this is probably why it has been associated with love and romance.

French pronunciation and ways of putting sentences together follow patterns particular, some may say peculiar, to the language. It also has constructions and vocabulary which are appropriate in some situations and not in others. The same is true in English. For example, in English when people write a formal letter, they carefully select conventional words and constructions which they organize in a standard manner. When they talk to friends, they use informal language to engage in more relaxed and spontaneous communication and are less attentive to the form of what they are saying; they are also inclined to include slang and colloquial expressions. It is important to be aware that, unlike in English, there is a correct and standard form of informal French. Using **tu**, for example, is not impolite or casual when used appropriately.

This is not a standard grammar book which tells you everything possible about the workings of the language – usually more than you want, or need, to know in the early stages of learning. It is intended to be the accessible guide you have been waiting for. It focuses on the recurrent challenges with which you as a beginner, intermediate or even quite advanced student are faced, and explains how to avoid making common errors. In order to bring to life some of the mistakes, language has been used in a variety of useful contexts.

If you are thinking of improving your French, or have decided to give the language another go, you are making the right choice in buying this book.

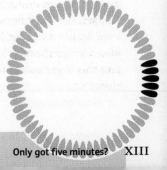

10 Only got ten minutes?

The French language

France is one of the most visited countries in the world. Its varied landscape, the beauty of its coastline, its colourful seasons, the charms of its old cities and the pace of life in its rural areas have all made France an attractive place to spend a holiday. For the last few decades, many British people have even decided to change their life and move to France, embracing both language and culture. An increasing number of adults are now learning French in order to integrate themselves better into their newly adopted community. Others find themselves thrust into a French working environment when their companies move or become multinational.

At the beginning of the twenty-first century France is still a largely rural country, with an even spread of population. Of course, historic cities (**les villes historiques**) and conurbations exist. Beyond them spreads spacious countryside (**la campagne**), not overcrowded but rarely deserted. The layout of the fields (**les champs**), the pattern of crops (**les cultures**) and woodlands (**les bois**), the grouping of the population in hamlets (**les hameaux**), villages (**les villages**) and towns (**les villes**), the local culinary specialities (**la cuisine régionale**), the local dialects (**le ch'ti**) and accents, all combine to proclaim the individuality of the many localities (**les pays**) which themselves contribute to the identity of the larger region and ultimately to the national identity. The country we see today has been created over the centuries by its inhabitants (**les habitants**), whose collective understanding and exploitation of the places (**les endroits**) they live in is expressed in every detail of the local landscape (**le paysage**). The capital (**la capitale**), Paris, is still considered as the political and cultural centre of France despite recent efforts to give regions more power (**la décentralisation**).

The diversity of France means that there isn't one single language common to and spoken by all French people without variation. As well as regional and cultural language differences, the French are also inclined to use slang and colloquial expressions to enrich their speech. All languages have constructions and vocabulary which are appropriate in some situations and not in others. For example, in English when we write formal letters, we carefully choose words and select conventional constructions which we then organize in a standard manner. When talking to friends, however, people use informal language to engage in more relaxed and spontaneous communication and are less attentive to the form of what they are saying; they often include slang and colloquial expressions in informal conversation. It is important to be aware that, unlike in English, there is a correct and standard form of informal French. **Tu** is not impolite or casual when used appropriately.

This book does not comment on regional particularities and accents found in France. Its authors have focused on what they consider to be the standard language, spoken and understood by most.

Learning any language cannot be dissociated from an appreciation of the culture of the country in which the language was born. Languages are the result of many years of historical change, both evolutionary and revolutionary. These changes affect the way we think about our world and are reflected in the ever-changing language we speak; French is no exception. As Raymond Williams wrote in 1976, words have been formed, altered, redefined, influenced, modified, confused and reinforced as the historical contexts in which they were applied have changed, to give us their current meaning and significance.

The emergence of new words is the result of such shifts. Recent globalization of not only economic principles but also of popular culture disseminated through the media has shaken traditional values deeply rooted in French ideology, behaviour and language. French is now heavily influenced by English and American cultures through music, technology, fashion, cinema and business practices, for example. English is becoming more and more visible in the language of the written press and on television. However, such transformation does not happen randomly. Newly formed language follows familiar rules of pronunciation and syntax, and is absorbed and embraced. English, although infiltrating and influencing the French language, does not in any way replace it. It is, therefore, important to understand and apply the good practice outlined in this book.

This is not a standard manual of grammar which tells you everything you could possibly wish to know about the workings of the French language – usually more than you want, or need, to know in the early stages of learning. It is intended as a handy, accessible guide to improve your ability to communicate using modern and authentic French. It highlights the recurrent mistakes which you as a beginner, intermediate or even quite advanced student are inclined to make, and explains how to avoid making them. In order to bring to life some of the mistakes, language has been used in a variety of useful contexts.

How to use this book

50 way to improve your French is not a series of lectures delivered by a stern, straight-backed academic standing at the blackboard, chalk in hand, imparting every possible detail about the workings of the French language – more than you may want, or need, to know in the early stages of learning. Instead, the intention of this book is to guide you through the linguistic fog which can envelop the student of a foreign language. It focuses on the real challenges with which you as a beginner, intermediate or even advanced student are faced, and tells you in simple terms what you can do to avoid making common mistakes in the future.

Do not feel that you are the only person who struggles to get the hang of the finer points of French; this is certainly not the case. Most errors are common to the majority of students and you, as you work through these pages, will come to understand and be able to avoid these mistakes. Making mistakes is part of the learning process, but if you confront them before they become entrenched it will be easier for you to make the necessary changes. The guide will help your language – and with it your confidence – to improve dramatically as a result.

The book consists of 50 short sections. Each one tackles a common mistake in pronunciation, structure or vocabulary. It presents the common mistake and gives the correct solution, often highlighting the fact that what 'feels right' for a speaker of English creates a trail of false hope and leads to mistakes that no native speaker would ever make or understand. Explanations are in plain English and use a minimum of grammatical terms; the few which are used are explained in the glossary. All examples used to illustrate a point are given in French with an English translation. The authors' insight boxes contain handy hints which may help you to keep the problem in perspective and remember the solution.

Whenever you encounter a problem, or perhaps when you're feeling a bit uncertain about a new situation, browse through the index and then read the relevant section of the book. You will understand why and where you are going wrong, and eventually you will find yourself automatically getting it right. It will have become second nature and you will have become a more natural, confident and fluent communicator in French.

You may find it helpful to follow this link: www.teachyourself.com. Here you will find a recording demonstrating some of the pronunciation mistakes highlighted in this book, a set of multiple choice questions to help you practise some of the language, as well as a set of informative articles about language and culture in France.

Sounding right

You may find it helpful to follow this link: www.teachyourself.com
Here you will find a recording demonstrating some of the
pronunciation mistakes highlighted in this section, and guidance to
avoid making them.

1 Vowel problems

In French, as in English, the mispronunciation of vowels ('a', 'e', 'i', 'o', 'u' and 'y') can be a source of communication problems. Note that in French the letter 'y' is considered a vowel, not a consonant, as it is called '**i grec**' (Greek 'i').

Have you ever asked for a chicken (**poule**) when you meant a jumper (**pull**), or have talked about hair (**cheveux**) when you meant horses (**chevaux**)?

▶ The sound 'au' is different from the sound 'eu'.
▶ The sound 'ou' is different from the sound 'u'.

DON'T CONFUSE 'AU' AND 'EU'

J'ai des chevaux courts. (sounds like 'shev<u>oh</u>') ?	*I have short horses.*
J'ai des cheveux courts. (sounds like 'shev<u>eu</u>' with the 'u' of 'f<u>ur</u>') ✓	*I have short hair.*
Est-il seul ? ('eu' sounds like the 'u' of 'f<u>ur</u>') ✓	*Is he alone?*
C'est un saule ? (sounds like the 'o' in 'solo') ✓	*Is it a willow?*

THE 'OU' AND 'U' PROBLEM

'*Sur*' *on* or '*sous*' *under*?

The sentences **Le sac est <u>sur</u> la table** (*The bag is <u>on</u> the table*) and **Le sac est <u>sous</u>** (sounds like 'soo') **la table** (*The bag is <u>under</u> the table*) are completely different. Where people expect to find the bag will depend on how well you pronounce **sur** or **sous**!

The sound 'u' does not exist in the English phonetic system. You have to create it in your mind. It does not give an 'oo' sound; it is more like the 'u' in 'Hugh' as you make a round shape with your mouth and you push your lips forward as if you were giving a kiss to someone.

le pullover (sounds like 'peullover') ✓

Now look at the following pairs of words and see how care must be taken to pronounce each word correctly.

la bûche (û as in 'Hugh')	*log*
la bouche ('booche')	*mouth*
le bourreau ('booro' as in 'solo')	*torturer, executioner*
le bureau (u as in 'Hugh')	*office, desk*
le cul (u as in 'Hugh')	*arse*
le cou ('coo')	*neck*
la roue ('roo')	*wheel*
la rue (u as in 'Hugh')	*street*
elle est russe (u as in 'Hugh')	*she is Russian*
elle est rousse ('roose')	*she is red-headed*
mes meilleurs vœux (œux as in 'fur')	*my best wishes*
mon meilleur veau (eau as in 'solo')	*my best veal*
un sac à deux (eux as in 'fur')	*one bag carried by two people*
un sac à dos (o as in 'solo')	*a backpack*

Insight

The French sounds 'an' and 'on', which are very similar, may also create problems. Take care to distinguish between:

Il arrive, con !	*He is on his way, you idiot!*
Il arrive quand ?	*When does he arrive?*

For help with the pronunciation of these vowel sounds in French, you may find it useful to listen to examples on the online recording which can be found following this link: www.teachyourself.com You may also find the section 'Simplified sound system' at the back of this book helpful (see page 138).

2 Consonant problems

In French the mispronunciation of the consonants 'c', 'g', 'h', 'j', 'q' and 'w', and spelling errors, can lead to misunderstandings – some just humorous and others particularly unfortunate!

PROBLEMS WITH 'S' AND 'SS': SOFT OR HARD?

In a restaurant, asking for **poison** (*poison*) or **désert** (*desert*) with a 'z' sound (as in '<u>z</u>oo'), instead of **poisson** (*fish*) or **dessert** (*dessert*) with an 's' sound (as in '<u>s</u>uper'), are easily made mistakes but ones which will be met with obvious surprise!

Another classic mistake is made when confusing **baiser** ('z' sound, *to kiss*, or the slang for *to make love*) with **baisser** ('s' sound, *to lower* or *to unwind*).

Il a bai<u>s</u>é la vitre. ✗	
Il a bai<u>ss</u>é la vitre. ✓	*He lowered the window.*
J'ai ca<u>s</u>é la voiture. ✗	
J'ai ca<u>ss</u>é la voiture. ✓	*I have broken the car.*

La casse (with an 's' sound) means *breakage*, but **la case** (pronounced with a 'z' sound) means *hut* or *cabin*.

4

Il a mis sa voiture à la ca__ss__e. ✗
Il a mis sa voiture à la ca__s__e. ✓   *He put his car in the hut.*

PROBLEMS WITH 'G'

Follow these rules to get it right every time:

- if the 'g' is followed by 'a', 'o' or 'u' it will sound hard (as in 'geek'): **gorge** (*throat*), **__G__ustave** or **gare** (*station*);

- if the 'g' is followed by 'e', 'i' or 'y' it will sound soft: **__G__ermaine**, **gel** (*frost*), **givre** (*hoarfrost*) (pronounced 'geevre') and **gym** (pronounced 'geem').

Now you know how to avoid the following common mispronunciations and can pronounce these words correctly:

gîte (*holiday cottage*) (pronounced 'geet') ✗
gîte (**g** as in 'germ', but a little softer) ✓
gestion (*management*) (**g** as in 'guest') ✗
gestion (**g** as in 'gesture') ✓
génécologue (*gynaecologist*) (**g** as in 'gesture') ✓

The rule is easy to apply!

PROBLEMS WITH 'C'

The 'c' rule is the same as the rule for 'g' described above:

- if the 'c' is followed by 'a', 'o' or 'u' it will sound hard, as in 'cat': **__c__atamaran**, **__c__olle** (*glue*) or **__c__ulotte** (*underpants*);
- the 'ç' always makes the sound soft, as in 'France': **Fran__ç__ais** or **ça va** (*I'm ok*);
- if the 'c' is followed by 'e', 'i' or 'y' the sound will be soft, e.g. **s__c__ène**, **__c__e__c__i**, **voi__c__i**, **__c__inq**, **__c__éleri** and **__c__ygne** (*swan*).

Now you can say with confidence in French **Ici git Givenchy** (*Here lies Givenchy*)!

3 Silent endings and -ent

Students have a tendency to pronounce the word ending -ent as the en- in **encore** or the -ent in **vent** wherever and whenever they read it in a word. Unfortunately, this is not always correct and it is a recurrent problem even at higher levels of proficiency.

WHEN DO WE PRONOUNCE '-ENT' IN THE SAME WAY AS '-ANT'?

The -ent in **vent** (*wind*) always sounds like the -ant in **étudiant** (*student*) or **enfant** (*child*), but does not sound like the **in-** or **im-** in **important** or **intelligent**.

Note that '**an**' is always pronounced as in **Antoine**, **chanson** (*song*) or **chanteur** (*singer*).

In the following examples the '**en**' is also pronounced like '**an**':

je vends/prends (with a silent '-ds')   *I sell/take*
il vend/prend (with a silent '-d')   *he sells/takes*

In our experience, this is not usually a problem for learners once they understand that the -t,-d and the -ds are always silent in such words unless they are followed by an **e** in the same way as the -s in **les stylos** will also be silent.

WHEN TO BE SIL...ENT

The -**ent** pronunciation problem occurs when in the present tense the -**ent** verb ending is used where several people are performing the action: here, the -**ent** ending is pronounced as though it were only -**e**.

ils marchent (sounds the same   *they are walking*
  as **il marche**, *he walks*)
ils travaillaient   *they used to work*
  (-**aient** pronounced as 'ai')

In the present tense the -**ent** verb ending is almost completely silent, or may sound like a weak and timid 'e' or even like the last letter of the word. For example:

ils parl(ent)	*they are speaking*
ils mar<u>ch</u>(ent)	*they are walking*
ils fini<u>ss</u>(ent)	*they are finishing*
ils ven<u>d</u>(ent)	*they are selling*

The above examples are in the present tense (what they do/are doing now), but if you need to use the imperfect (what they used to do) or the conditional (what they would do) tenses, the same rule applies. Look at the following examples:

ils travaillaient (the final syllable sounds like 'ay')	*they used to work*
ils travailleraient (the final syllable sounds like 'ay')	*they would work*

As you can see, in these tenses the ending -**ent** is completely silent.

If the -**ent** ending is pronounced:

▶ it either changes the meaning altogether (see Chapter 27a);
▶ or the person listening to you will think you are using the -**ons** ending to your verb, e.g. **nous écout<u>ons</u>** and **nous voul<u>ons</u>**.

Insight

The sound 'ai' is very close to the sound of the vowel 'a' in English. To make the French 'ai' sound perfectly, just open your mouth more by making an oval shape with your mouth. The sound comes from the back of your mouth, not from the front as in English.

4 Numbers count

The pronunciation of the numbers **deux** (2), **trois** (3), **cinq** (5), **six** (6), **huit** (8), **neuf** (9), **dix** (10), **vingt** (20) and **cent** (100) can catch you out! Numbers, by their very essence, have to be accurate and this goes for their pronunciation too.

'DEUX', 'SIX' AND 'DIX'

These three numbers end with the letter 'x'. They sound different in different contexts, as shown below:

deux omelettes (x of deu<u>x</u> giving a 'z' sound)
dix maisons (di<u>x</u> with a silent '**x**')

This is how it works:

▶ The 'x' in si<u>x</u> or di<u>x</u> is usually pronounced as an 's', and the 'x' of deu<u>x</u> is silent when said in isolation.

Combien de livres as-tu ?	*How many books have you got?*
Deux, six ou dix ? (sounds like 'de', 'see-s', 'dee-s')	*Two, six or ten?*

▶ The 'x' in deu<u>x</u>, si<u>x</u> and di<u>x</u> is pronounced 'z' when followed by a word beginning with a vowel ('a', 'e', 'i', 'o', 'u' and 'y').

deux ans (the 'x' is pronounced 'z')	*two years*
six ans (the 'x' is pronounced 'z')	*six years*
dix ans (the 'x' is pronounced 'z')	*ten years*

▶ However, the 'x' is always silent when the next word begins with a consonant.

deux maisons (with a silent '**x**')	*two houses*

'CINQ', 'HUIT' AND 'NEUF'

The 'q' of cinq is also never silent, but instead is pronounced like a 'k'.

The 'h' in huit is always silent and the 't' is always pronounced. The 'ui' in huit sounds like 'wee' in *we*.

The 'f' at the end of neuf is never silent, or it would sound like nœud (*knot*).

'VINGT' AND 'CENT'

Since the introduction of the euro in 2000, many French media presenters have repeatedly mispronounced cent and vingt before the word euro:

cent euros (cent euros with a silent 't') ✘

They should be sounding the 't':

cent euros (cent euros with the sound 't') ✔

The 't' of cent and vingt and the 's' in trois are never silent when followed by a word beginning with a vowel, and are usually silent when the following word starts with a consonant or phantom 'h' (see Chapter 9), so the practice is similar to that described for deux and dix.

Insight
Regional variations in accent throughout France can result in different pronunciation. In the south of France, in particular, the 't' at the end of cent may be sounded, and the 'z/s' sound for 'x' at the end of deux, six and dix may be exaggerated.

5 Accent deficit disorder

The four French accents for vowels and one for a consonant may not only change the pronunciation of the letter they pair with but also their meanings.

Le fromage est sale. ✗	*The cheese is dirty.*
Le fromage est salé. ✓	*The cheese is salty.*

An incorrect or missing accent is a spelling mistake just as incorrect as missing out a letter would be in an English word. The only exceptions to this rule are capital letters, which are often left unaccented.

THE ACUTE ACCENT

The acute accent (**accent aigu**) is only found on an 'e'. It often indicates that an 's' used to follow that vowel in old French and may help you to work out the meaning, e.g. **étudiant** (*student*).

THE GRAVE ACCENT

The grave accent (**accent grave**) can be found on the letters 'a', 'e' or 'u'. On the letters 'a' and 'u' the grave accent usually serves to distinguish between words spelt the same way but with different meanings or functions. For example:

ou (*or*) but **où** (*where*)   **à** (*to, at*) but **a** (*has*)

THE CIRCUMFLEX ACCENT

The circumflex accent (**accent circonflexe**) can be found on the letters 'a', 'e', 'i', 'o' and 'u'. The circumflex accent usually indicates that an 's' used to follow that vowel, e.g. **forêt** (*forest*).

It also serves to distinguish between words spelt the same way but with different meanings or functions. For example:

du (contraction of **de** + **le**) but **j'ai dû**... *I had to...*

THE DIERESIS

The dieresis or **tréma** can be seen on an 'e', 'i' and 'u'. It is used when two vowels are next to each other and both must be pronounced, e.g. **naïve** ('na eev'), **Noël** ('no el'), **égoïste** ('ego eest'), **Joëlle** ('jo el').

A common error made by English speakers which confuses the French is: **J'ai un citron** (*I have got a lemon*, pronounced 'ci-tron'), instead of **J'ai une Citroën** (*I have got a Citroën*, pronounced ci-tro-en).

THE CEDILLA

The cedilla (**cédille**) is found only on the letter 'c'. It changes a hard 'c' sound (like 'k') into a soft 'c' sound (like 's'), e.g. **garçon** ('garsson').

Here are a few words which often cause problems:

âge	*age*	**âgé**	*old*
Marie		**marié**	*married*
entre	*between*	**entré**	*entered*
vous êtes	*you are*	**des étés**	*some summers*
(la) ferme	*(the) farm*	**fermé**	*closed*

Insight
Even when sending text messages accents cannot be avoided!

'Jregrt dpartir kom ça. G pa c 1 supr soiré' means:

Je regrette de partir comme ça.	*I was sorry to leave like that.*
J'ai passé une super soirée.	*I had a lovely evening.*

6 Capital letters can lead to capital errors!

Many words that are spelt with a capital letter in English are not in French. Here are a few basic rules to follow to avoid making some common errors.

The following words are <u>not</u> capitalized in French as they are in English.

DAYS OF THE WEEK AND MONTHS OF THE YEAR

Lundi, Mardi, Mercredi... ✗
lundi, mardi, mercredi... ✓   *Monday, Tuesday, Wednesday*
Janvier, Février, Mars... ✗
janvier, février, mars... ✓   *January, February, March*

PLACE NAMES

Rue Emile Zola ✗
rue Emile Zola ✓   *Emile Zola Street*
l'Océan Pacifique ✗
l'océan Pacifique ✓   *the Pacific Ocean*
Le Mont Blanc ✗
Le mont Blanc ✓   *Mont Blanc*

NATIONALITIES

French adjectives that refer to nationalities are not capitalized, but proper nouns (e.g. a Frenchman, the Swiss) are.

Je suis Américain. ✗
Je suis américain. ✓   *I'm American.*
C'est un Américain qui aime   *He is an American*
  la France. ✓   *who loves France.*

LANGUAGES

**Je parle le Français, l'Anglais,
  le Russe,** ✗
**Je parle le français, l'anglais
  et le russe.** ✓   *I speak French, English and
  Russian.*

POINTS OF THE COMPASS

Direction words such as **nord** (*north*), **sud** (*south*), **est** (*east*) and
ouest (*west*) and all their possible combinations (**nord-ouest**, etc.)
are not capitalized.

**Nous avons roulé pendant
  5 kilomètres vers le Nord.** ✗
**Nous avons roulé pendant
  5 kilomètres vers le nord.** ✓   *We drove north for 5 kilometres.*

However, capitalization is compulsory when indicating the name
of a place.

Beware: capital letters can change the meaning of a word!

Il habite dans le nord.   *He lives in <u>the north</u>.* (i.e. more
generally and relatively in the
north)

Il habite dans le Nord.   *He lives in <u>the North</u>.* (i.e. the
administrative division or
département 59)

Insight

Capital letters can be left without accents and many French
people do not bother to add them, especially when sending
text messages, but they must be used when there is potential
ambiguity.

BISCUITS SALES   *dirty crackers*
BISCUITS SALÉS   *salty crackers*

7 Mission impossible: how to pronounce words beginning with a vowel + n/m

PRONOUNCING 'IN(N)-' AND 'IM(M)-'

Is the sound short, long or nasal? Sounds like mission impossible!

The pronunciation of words which begin **in**(n)- or **im**(m)- in French can cause difficulties! There are a lot of these types of words, and they are often spelt almost the same and mean the same as in English. It is hardly surprising that students find themselves tempted to pronounce them as they would in English with a short vowel sound, as in _international_ or _important_. This is not a vowel sound which exists in French, so can't be right, but there is a sure-fire way to work out the correct pronunciation.

To pronounce these words correctly in French, the first step is to stop and think which letter comes after the **in**(n)- or **im**(m)-.

▶ If that letter is a vowel ('a', 'e', 'i', 'o' or 'u'), then the first syllable is pronounced with a long 'i' sound, as in the English word _seen_ or _seem_. It works every time! For example:

in**a**ctif	(sounds like '_ee_nactif')
im**a**ge	(sounds like '_ee_mage')
in**é**vitable	(sounds like '_ee_névitable')
imm**é**diat	(sounds like '_ee_mmédia')
inn**o**cent	(sounds like '_ee_nocent')
imm**o**ral	(sounds like '_ee_mmoral')

▶ If, however, the letter which follows the **in**- is a consonant, then that sound is pronounced in a nasal way, as in _anxious_. After **im**- it is pronounced as the 'am' in _ham_:

in**f**ormation	(sounds like '_an_formation')
im**p**ortant	(sounds like '_am_portant')
in**s**tant	(sounds like '_an_stant')
in**t**act	(sounds like '_an_tact')

PRONOUNCING WORDS BEGINNING WITH OTHER VOWELS AND FOLLOWED BY '-M' OR '-N'

In this group are words beginning with the following letters: am(m)-, an(n)-, em-, en(n)-, om(n)-, -on- and un-.

▶ The pronunciation of these words depends on the letter which immediately follows. If it is a vowel, then the initial letter of the word ('a', 'e', 'o' or 'u') will be pronounced as follows:

amitié, animal	(initial 'a' sounds like the 'a' in 'cat')
éminent	(initial 'é' sounds like the 'a' in 'gate')
ennemi	(initial 'e' sounds like the 'e' in 'get')
omission	(initial 'o' sounds like the 'o' in 'top')
uniforme	(initial 'u' sounds like the 'u' in 'include')

Note that there are a few exceptions to this rule, such as **ennuyer** (*to bore*) and **emmener** (*to take*) where the pronunciation is as in 'song', and **immangeable** (*inedible*), where the pronunciation is as in 'anxious'.

▶ If the next letter is a consonant, then the initial letter has a nasal sound. For example:

angle	(with a nasal 'o' sound, as in 'song')
embrasser	(with a nasal 'o' sound, as in 'song')
ombre	(with a nasal 'o' sound, as in 'umbrella')

Insight

There are, of course, many French words which begin with a vowel and which are followed by a consonant other than 'n' or 'm', and these are pronounced as follows:

abricot, adorable,	(initial 'a' sounds like the 'a' in 'cat')
effort	(initial 'e' sounds like the 'e' in 'get')
illégal	(initial 'i' sounds like the 'ee' in 'seen')
obstacle	(initial 'o' sounds like the 'o' in 'top')
utile	(initial 'u' sounds like the 'u' in 'Hugh')
élégant	(initial 'é' sounds like the 'a' in 'gate')

8 Don't get stressed about stress!

WHERE DOES THE STRESS FALL COMFORTABLY?

Stress is part and parcel of everyday life, but learning how to speak French doesn't need to make you anxious! When it comes to languages, 'stress' means using emphasis (in terms of loudness, pitch or length) on one syllable or part of a phrase.

Syllables are the small combinations of sounds that divide a word up naturally as we say them; so, for example, the word *authentic* has three syllables: '*au-then-tic*'. As native English speakers, we know how stress falls within these words; just try saying *au-<u>then</u>-tic* landing heavily on the underlined syllable. It just doesn't sound like English!

The French word **authentique** (*authentic*) also has three syllables **au-then-<u>tique</u>**, and the stress falls on the final syllable: **tique**. Syllable stress is indicated here by underlining those letters on which the stress falls. (To listen to examples on the online audio recording, follow the link <u>www.teachyourself.com</u>)

Consider the word *improbable* – spelt the same way in English and in French, and with identical meaning.

In English we say *im-<u>pro</u>-ba-ble* wherever the word is placed in the sentence. But in French different rules apply, which makes knowing where to place the stress much more predictable.

1 When you are pronouncing individual words, the stress falls on the last syllable containing a vowel which is pronounced. So, for example, in French:

improb<u>ab</u>le ✓

The unaccented vowel 'e' at the end of a French word does not count as a syllable.

2 Let's look at a few different examples:

thon (*tuna*)   This word has one syllable.

from-age (*cheese*)   This word has two syllables. The stress
                              falls on the last syllable.

ab-ri-cots (*apricots*)   This word has three syllables. The stress
                              falls on the last syllable.

su-cre (*sugar*)   This word has one syllable – the
                              unaccented 'e' doesn't count.

Words like **oui** (*yes*), **lui** (*him*) and **Louis** are words of one syllable only. So, if you ever say '**Oui**, c'est **lui**, le verita**ble Louis**!' (*Yes, it's him, the real Louis!*), you will have used only eight syllables and four stresses!

3 In French sentences, only the syllable which comes at the end of a group of words belonging naturally together is accentuated.

Ils sont **bons, ce** fromage **et ce** thon,
  mais ces abricots **sont** agréables
  même avec **du** sucre. ✗

Il sont **bons** — ce fromage — et ce   *This cheese and this tuna are*
  thon — mais ces abricots — sont   *good, but these apricots are*
  agréables — même avec du sucre. ✓   *nice, even with sugar.*

....

Insight

Stress is not very heavy in French because it is not as crucial as in some languages, where a wrongly placed stress can change the meaning of a word.

Don't be put off! Stress in French is far less stressful than in English which, as your mother tongue, you learned without having to get 'stressed about stress'!

....

9 Contractions without pain and the influence of the 'h' factor

In English, linking one word with another using an apostrophe to replace a letter (e.g. *we're* instead of *we are*) is optional. These contractions, or short forms, tend to indicate less formal communication, and are more common in speech than in writing.

In French, contractions, where necessary, are compulsory. They must be made in speech and in writing.

The weak 'e' of c<u>e</u>, d<u>e</u>, j<u>e</u>, l<u>e</u> (and the 'a' of l<u>a</u>), m<u>e</u>, n<u>e</u>, qu<u>e</u>, s<u>e</u> and t<u>e</u> is dropped and the resulting c', d', j', l', m', n', qu', s' and t' attach themselves to any word beginning with the vowel which follows.

c<u>e</u> est ✗	c'est ✓	*it is*
beaucoup d<u>e</u> animaux ✗	beaucoup d'animaux ✓	*lots of animals*
j<u>e</u> ai ✗	j'ai ✓	*I have*
l<u>e</u> ami, l<u>a</u> amie ✗	l'ami, l'amie ✓	*the (boy)friend, the (girl)friend*
je m<u>e</u> ennuie ✗	je m'ennuie ✓	*I'm bored*
ce n<u>e</u> est pas ✗	ce n'est pas ✓	*it isn't*
parce qu<u>e</u> il ✗	parce qu'il ✓	*because he*
il s<u>e</u> ennuie ✗	il s'ennuie ✓	*he's bored*
je t<u>e</u> ennuie ✗	je t'ennuie ✓	*I'm boring you*

THE 'H' FACTOR

French people never need to learn to produce 'h' in their own language and they have to practise huffing and puffing in order to create it when they learn English! Ironically, though, 'h' has not disappeared from French spelling and it controls, like a tyrant, what happens to the words positioned immediately before it.

There are in fact are two kinds of letter 'h'– mute (**muet**) and aspirated (**aspiré**) – despite their silence.

When you learn a word beginning with the letter 'h', it's a good idea to try to remember what kind of 'h' it is because:

▶ if it is mute it has no power at all over the preceding word; it behaves just as if the word started with the vowel which follows:

homme (m.) *man* **l'homme** (pronounced 'lom') *the man*
habitude (f.) *habit* **l'habitude** (pronounced 'labitude') *the habit*

▶ if it is aspirated, despite beginning with a vowel sound there are no contractions (what a relief!); grammatically, it's as if the 'h' were a sounding consonant.

homard (m.) *lobster* **le homard** (pronounced *the lobster*
'le omard')
haine (f.) *hatred* **la haine** (pronounced *(the) hatred*
'la aine')

Most 'h's are mute. Here are a few more examples:

comme d'habitude ✓ (pronounced '... dabitude') *as usual*
j'habite ✓ (pronounced 'jabite') *I live*
l'heure ✓ (pronounced 'leure') *the time*
je m'habille ✓ (pronounced 'je mabille') *I get dressed*
l'histoire ✓ (pronounced 'listoire') *the story,*
  the history

Relatively few 'h's are aspirated, but here are some examples:

le hamburger *the hamburger*
le hasard *(the) chance*

Insight
Pronounce a word beginning with the letter 'h' after a contraction as if the 'h' were not there at all. Just go straight to the first vowel sound, with no hesitation; e.g. **j'hésite** (I *hesitate*) is pronounced with just two syllables: **j'hé-site**.

10 Liaisons – some of them are dangerous – and how to pronounce **plus**

WHEN TO FORM LIAISONS

When we speak a familiar language, words flow naturally into each other and it is difficult to hear where one word ends and another begins. A phrase can sound just like one long, continuous word. The links we make between words are called 'liaisons' and they occur in French between a word which ends in a consonant which is normally silent, and one which begins with a vowel (or a mute 'h').

Les_enfants sont_heureux quand_ils voient leurs_amis et ils peuvent partir_ensemble pour_aller jouer. ✓

Children are happy when they meet their friends and they can go and play together.

If you pause between each word in a sentence, the sentence will not flow and the meaning may be lost. It just sounds like a robotic list of disconnected words.

One important exception to the liaison rule is underlined in the example above:

▶ the 't' on the end of the French word **et** is always silent.

With words ending **-d** (e.g. **quand**) the 'd' sounds like a 't' before a vowel.

Here are a few more examples showing where liaisons are required:

Prends un ballon, Marie ! ✗
Prends_un ballon, Marie ! ✓   *Take a ball, Marie!*
Allez y tous ! ✗
Allez_y tous ! ✓   *Off you go, all of you.*

Les_enfants vont_au stade. ✓   *The children go to the sports ground.*
Ils reviennent_enfin quand('t')_on   *They come back when they*
  les_appelle. ✓   *are called.*

'PLUS' *MORE* OR 'PLUS' *NO MORE*?

Not knowing when the 's' in **plus** is silent and when it is not could mean that you miss out on many good things...

Je n'ai plus de tomates.   *I have no more tomatoes.*
  (**plus** with a silent 's') ✓

The rule is simple:

▶ if you want more of something, the 's' in **plus** is pronounced.
▶ if **plus** is used to say that there is no more, or that you have had enough, its 's' is silent.

   Je n'en ai plus.   *I have no more.*
   Vous en avez plus ?   *Do you have any more?*

When invited for dinner, if your host asks whether you would like **plus** or **encore**, he or she is offering you a second helping. Just stick to this rule and you will never be deprived of anything!

Insight
You may meet French people who do not follow the standard rules of liaison, including presenters on TV. In case of ambiguity, just ask for confirmation, by saying, for example, '**Plus** (+) **ou plus** (–)?', and the problem will be solved to the amusement of all!

Getting the structure right

11 Adjectives – you don't have **carte blanche!**

WHERE TO PUT ADJECTIVES

The usual position for an adjective is after the item it describes.

un livre intéressant   *an interesting book*
un film ennuyeux   *a boring film*

This is not always the case, however, and the exceptions include some of the most common adjectives in use.

Tu as vu ce melon gros ? ✗
Tu as vu ce gros melon ? ✓   *Have you seen this big melon?*
Quelles tomates belles ! ✗
Quelles belles tomates ! ✓   *What beautiful tomatoes!*

Watch out for the following common adjectives which are usually placed <u>before</u> the noun. This is then what they mean when you do:

beau, belle	*good-looking*	**bon(ne)**	*good*
grand(e)	*big, tall*	**gros(se)**	*big, fat*
jeune	*young*	**joli(e)**	*pretty, nice*
nouveau, nouvelle	*new*	**petit(e)**	*small*
propre	*own*	**sale**	*nasty*

SOME ADJECTIVES CAN CHANGE THEIR MEANING: 'GRAND', 'SALE', 'PROPRE' AND 'NOUVEAU'

As you know, French nouns and adjectives have to know their place and agree with each other in order to be in harmony (see Chapter 20). Some adjectives, however, are fickle and can be used <u>before or after</u> a noun; the meaning of the adjective may change, depending upon its position in the sentence. (Be especially careful when you use the word **sale** (*dirty*) – there is nothing wrong with some good honest dirt, but if you put its French equivalent in the wrong place in the sentence it could be very insulting to the person concerned!)

Here are some examples:

Le marchand de fleurs est un homme grand.	*The flower seller is a <u>tall</u> man.*
Son père était maire de la ville; c'était un <u>grand homme</u>.	*His father was mayor of the town; he was a <u>great</u> man.*
La <u>nouvelle vendeuse</u> est très amusante.	*The <u>new</u> (succeeding) stallholder is very funny.*
Regarde ! Il y a des <u>pommes de terre nouvelles</u> chez le marchand de fruits et légumes.	*There are <u>new</u> (appearing for the first time) potatoes on the fruit and vegetable stall.*
Ses légumes viennent de son <u>propre jardin</u> potager.	*His vegetables come from his <u>own</u> vegetable garden.*
Il vend des <u>salades propres</u>.	*He sells <u>clean</u> lettuces.*
Tu as vu les <u>mains sales</u> qu'il a ?	*Have you seen what <u>dirty</u> hands he's got?*
On dit que, malgré ses bons légumes, c'est un <u>sale type</u>.	*People say he's an <u>unpleasant</u> character.*

Insight

There is a certain logic to the normal placing of an adjective <u>after</u> the noun it describes since adjectives are, after all, in most cases additional extras. If the adjective is omitted, the sentence will usually still make sense, even though it may lack interesting detail; e.g. **j'ai vu un chien (blanc)** (*I saw a (white) dog*).

USING TWO ADJECTIVES

If you want to use two adjectives, both of which belong in front of the noun, you put them side by side where they belong. When you use two adjectives after a noun, as is more usual, you link them with **et** (*and*), and when using two adjectives, one of which belongs before and one after the noun, you leave them in their rightful place:

Je vais acheter ces <u>jolies petites</u> fleurs.	*I am going to buy these pretty little flowers.*
Je vais prendre aussi des pêches <u>blanches et jaunes</u>.	*I'm also going to have some white and yellow peaches.*
Ces <u>petites</u> fraises <u>mûres</u> ont l'air <u>délicieuses</u>.	*These little ripe strawberries look delicious.*

12 Negatives – where do the **ne** and the **pas** belong?

Not is the word used in English to negate a statement or a question. Informally, we usually use the shortened form *-n't*. To do so we have to introduce the word *do* in the present and *did* in the past tenses. For example: *I <u>don't</u> swim, I <u>didn't</u> swim.*

NOT 'NE...PAS'

In French we have to deal with the two negative words **ne** and **pas** – double trouble! When we use a single verb in a sentence, the **ne** is placed before the verb and the **pas** is placed after the verb. Unlike in English, the verb *to do* (**faire**) does not appear in any shape or form.

Je <u>ne</u> nage <u>pas</u>.   *I do not swim. I can't/don't swim. I am not swimming.*

When we use two verbs next to each other, as in *I do not <u>want</u> to <u>go</u> on holiday*, it's the first verb which is bracketed by ne...pas.

Je <u>ne</u> veux <u>pas</u> partir en vacances.   *I don't want to go on holiday.*
Nous <u>n</u>'allons <u>pas</u> prendre l'avion.   *We are not going to fly.*
Donc, nous <u>ne</u> sommes <u>pas</u> partis   *So, we didn't go on holiday.*
en vacances.

In this last example the **ne** and **pas** enclose the first of the two verbs comprising the past tense (in this case, **être**); this is the golden rule.

NEVER 'NE...JAMAIS', NO LONGER 'NE...PLUS' AND NOTHING 'NE...RIEN'

Double trouble again as the **ne** and either **jamais, plus** or **rien** are needed to complete the negative sentence. The rules for positioning are the same as for **ne...pas**.

ne…jamais	never
ne…plus	no longer
ne…rien	nothing
Il **ne** part <u>jamais</u> en vacances avec cette amie.	*He never goes on holiday with this friend.*
Ils **n'**ont <u>rien</u> fait cette année.	*They didn't do anything this year.*
Ils n'ont plus d'amis à l'étranger.	*They no longer have any friends abroad.*

NOBODY 'NE…PERSONNE' IS DIFFERENT

| ne…personne | nobody |

These negative words go before and after the verb, as usual, when you use the present tense.

| Il **n'**invite <u>personne</u> à bord. | *He doesn't welcome anyone on board.* |

Note the positioning of **personne** when you use the past tense:

| Il **n'**a invité <u>personne</u> à bord. | *He hasn't invited anyone on board.* |

Likewise, where there is <u>more than one verb</u> involved **personne** must be positioned after the second verb:

| Il **ne** va inviter <u>personne</u> à bord. | *He isn't going to welcome anyone on board.* |

Insight

To say '(n)either…(n)or', use **ne…ni…ni**: e.g. **Je n'ai ni froid ni chaud** (*I am neither hot nor cold*); **Je n'aime ni le soleil ni le vent** (*I don't like either the sun or the wind/I like neither sun nor wind*).

13a Direct object pronouns – get them sorted!

PROBLEMS WITH DIRECT OBJECT PRONOUNS 'LE', 'LA', 'LES', 'ME', 'TE', 'NOUS' AND 'VOUS'

A pronoun is a word used to replace a noun. A direct object pronoun replaces the direct object (i.e. the person or thing on the receiving end of the action) in a sentence when it is clear who or what is being referred to, e.g. *I buy <u>the book</u>* → *I buy <u>it</u>*; *I order <u>my clothes</u> online* → *I order <u>them</u> online*; *I like <u>Gill</u>* → *I like <u>her</u>*. The French direct object pronouns are: **me** (*me*), **te** (*you*), **le** (*him, it*), **la** (*her, it*), **les** (*them*), **nous** (*us*) and **vous** (*you*).

There are two particular problems for learners of French with using direct object pronouns:

▸ choosing the correct pronoun with which to replace the noun, and remembering not to confuse direct with indirect object pronouns (the people in a sentence <u>to</u> or <u>for</u> whom the action occurs, e.g. je <u>lui</u> parle (*I am talking <u>to him</u>*) (see Chapter 14);
▸ knowing where to position the direct object pronoun.

Here are a few common mistakes:

Linda voit John/Mary.   *Linda sees John/Mary.*
1 Linda voit il/elle. ✗
2 Linda voit lui. ✗
3 Linda lui voit. ✗
4 Linda <u>le</u> voit. ✓   *Linda sees <u>him</u>.*
5 Linda <u>la</u> voit. ✓   *Linda sees <u>her</u>.*

WHICH PRONOUN?

Look at the above examples.

1 John and Mary cannot be replaced with **il** or **elle** since Linda is the main named actor (i.e. the subject of the sentence).
2, 3 Using **lui** instead would mean 'to John' or 'to Mary', which would not make sense here.

4 John, therefore, is replaced by the direct object pronoun **le** because John is on the receiving end of the action (i.e. he is just the object).

5 Likewise, Mary is replaced by **la**.

If Linda had watched television, football or the children instead of John, **la télévision** would have been replaced by **la**:

Linda regarde <u>la télé</u>.	*Linda watches (the) TV.*
Linda <u>la</u> regarde.	*Linda watches <u>it</u>.*

If Linda had watched football instead of the TV, **le football** would have become **le**:

Linda regarde <u>le football</u>.	*Linda watches (the) football.*
Linda <u>le</u> regarde avec son mari.	*Linda watches <u>it</u> with her husband.*

If Linda had watched the children instead of the TV or the football, **les enfants** would have become **les**:

Linda regarde <u>les enfants</u> jouer.	*Linda watches the children play.*
Linda <u>les</u> regarde jouer.	*Linda is watching <u>them</u> play.*

WHERE TO POSITION DIRECT OBJECT PRONOUNS

The placing of **le, la, les, me, te, se, nous** and **vous** is in fact straightforward: all these direct object pronouns come just <u>after</u> the person who is doing the action and <u>before</u> the verb indicating the action.

Pierre regarde Julie.	*Pierre looks at Julie.*
Pierre regarde la. ✗	
Pierre <u>la</u> regarde. ✓	*Pierre watches <u>her</u>.*
Il voit tu. ✗	
Il voit te. ✗	
Il <u>te</u> voit. ✓	*He sees <u>you</u> (informal).*
Je vois vous lundi. ✗	
Je <u>vous</u> vois lundi. ✓	*I will see <u>you</u> (formal) on Monday.*
Nous <u>vous</u> voyons. ✓	*We see <u>you</u>.*
Vous <u>nous</u> voyez. ✓	*You see <u>us</u>.*
Ils <u>les</u> voient. ✓	*They see <u>them</u>.*

13b More possibilities with direct object pronouns

DIRECT OBJECT PRONOUNS IN THE PAST

Even when used in sentences in the past tense, direct pronouns **le,
la, les, me, te, nous** and **vous** are always placed after the person
performing the action, whether this person has a name or is
replaced by a subject pronoun (**je, tu, il…**).

J'ai vu John.	*I saw John.*
J'ai vu lui. ✗	
J'ai vu le. ✗	
Je l'ai vu. ✓	*I saw <u>him</u>.*

Lui is the wrong pronoun (indirect) in this sentence and **le** is badly
placed in the above sentences.

J'ai vu <u>Marie</u>.	*I saw Marie.*
J'ai vu elle. ✗	
J'ai vu la. ✗	
Je l'ai vue. ✓	*I saw <u>her</u>.*

Elle is the wrong pronoun (subject pronoun) and **la** should be
placed before **ai** (le/la + ai = l'ai).

DIRECT OBJECT PRONOUNS AND EXPRESSING PREFERENCES

When **aimer** (*to like*), **préférer** (*to prefer*) and **détester** (*to hate*)
are used to describe how much you like, prefer or hate doing
something, the pronouns must be placed before the second verb.

Il aime regarder <u>la télévision</u>.	*He likes to watch (the) television.*
Il la aime regarder ✗	
Il aime <u>la</u> regarder. ✓	*He likes to watch <u>it</u>.*

DIRECT OBJECT PRONOUNS AND FUTURE INTENTIONS

As with **aimer** (*to like*), when expressing what someone is going to do in the future, direct object pronouns are positioned before the second verb.

Julie, je vais voir la lundi. ✗
Julie, je vais <u>la</u> voir lundi. ✓   *Julie, I am going to see <u>her</u> on Monday.*

<u>Ce livre</u>, je vais <u>le</u> commander immédiatement.   *I will order this book straight away.*

DESIRES, OBLIGATIONS AND ABILITIES

These follow the same pattern, with direct object pronouns coming before the second verb. Look at these examples:

<u>Ce film</u>, il le veut voir lundi. ✗
<u>Ce film</u>, il veut <u>le</u> voir lundi. ✓   *He wants to see that film on Monday.*

<u>Cette règle</u>, nous devons <u>la</u> comprendre !   *We must understand that rule.*

<u>Les pronoms directs</u>, vous pouvez <u>les</u> utiliser maintenant !   *You can now use direct pronouns!*

<u>Les noms des étudiants</u>, il faut <u>les</u> mémoriser.   *The student's names have to be memorized.*

....

Insight

Pronouns always come after **pour** (*in order to*):

Ce livre, je vais le commander immédiatement pour le lire avant la fin de la semaine.   *I will order this book immediately in order to read it before the end of the week.*

....

14 Sort out your direct from your indirect object pronouns!

WHAT ARE INDIRECT OBJECT PRONOUNS?

In this sentence there is both a direct and an indirect object: *James gives a present to his sister*. James is the subject of the sentence who gives the present (direct object) to his sister (indirect object). It's the same in French: **James donne un cadeau à sa sœur.**

In English you often precede the indirect object with *to*, and in French with **à**.

The indirect objects can be replaced with pronouns, just the same as direct objects (see Chapters 13a, 13b). They stand in for the people in a sentence to or for whom the action of the verb occurs and imply that there is an interaction between the person who performs the action and the person to or for whom it is being performed: **James lui donne un cadeau** (*James gives a present to her*).

The French indirect object pronouns are: **me** (*me*), **te** (*you*), **lui** (*him, her*), **nous** (*us*), **vous** (*you*) and **leur** (*them*).

WHERE TO PUT INDIRECT OBJECT PRONOUNS

Like direct object pronouns, French indirect object pronouns (**me, te, lui, nous, vous** and **leur**) are usually placed <u>after</u> the person, or people, who perform the action and <u>in front of</u> the verb or the action. Look at the following common errors.

Je parle à la fille.	*I speak to the girl.*
Je parle lui. ✗	
Je parle à lui. ✗	
Je parle à il. ✗	
Je <u>lui</u> parle. ✓	*I'm speaking <u>to her</u>.*
Il parle aux enfants.	*He speaks to the children.*
Il parle à elles. ✗	
Il parle à les. ✗	

Il les parlent. ✗
Il leur parle. ✓   *He speaks to them.*

Me and **te** change to **m'** and **t'** respectively in front of a vowel or mute 'h' (see Chapter 9).

WHICH VERBS REQUIRE INDIRECT OBJECT PRONOUNS?

In English, the word *to* which follows *to talk* indicates that what comes next will be an indirect object. There are many verbs requiring the use of indirect object pronouns **me, te, lui, nous, vous** and **leur**, just as they do in English:

parler à quelqu'un	*to talk to someone*
envoyer un email/une lettre à quelqu'un	*to send an email/a letter to someone*
répondre à quelqu'un	*to reply to someone*
ordonner à quelqu'un	*to demand from someone*
téléphoner à quelqu'un	*to telephone someone*
demander à quelqu'un	*to ask someone*
poser une question à quelqu'un	*to ask someone a question*
commander à quelqu'un	*to order something from someone (e.g. by mail order, or in a restaurant)*
offrir à quelqu'un	*to give (e.g. a present) to someone*
acheter à quelqu'un	*to buy for (or from) someone*

All these verbs require another person to successfully complete the interaction. Learners often make mistakes with these verbs, ignoring the *to* (**à**) as they would in English.

Je téléphone à Paul.	*I telephone Paul.*
Je lui téléphone.	*I telephone him.*
Il pose la question à sa femme.	*He asks his wife the question.*
Il lui pose la question.	*He asks her the question.*
Elle répond à son mari.	*She replies to her husband.*
Elle lui répond.	*She replies to him.*
Nous envoyons un mail aux directeurs.	*We send an email to the managers.*
Nous leur envoyons un mail.	*We send them an email.*

15 Y and en, the pronouns for 'there' and 'some of it'

The French pronouns **y** and **en** are so tiny that one might think their function in a sentence insignificant, but in fact quite the opposite is true. They are both very important and create problems for learners.

Broadly speaking, **y** replaces a place (e.g. Paris) and **en** a number of things (e.g. **des tomates,** *tomatoes*) or people (e.g. **des enfants,** *children*).

HOW TO USE 'Y'

Je vais à Paris. Je vais <u>là</u> ce week-end ! ✗

Je vais à Paris. J'<u>y</u> vais ce week-end ! ✓ — *I am going to Paris. I'm going (there) this weekend!*

Insight

Je vais **là-bas ce week-end** sounds just as authentic as J'y vais **ce week-end.** You will hear French people saying **Je vais là-bas** in familiar speech, although **J'y vais** is strictly speaking correct. Note, however, that **On va là** (*We are going there*) is correct usage, and makes the distinction between this and **On y va !** (*Let's go!*)

Y refers to a place previously mentioned or an implied place; it is normally translated by *there* in English. **Y** usually replaces a phrase beginning with something like **à, chez,** or **dans** but sometimes the phrase introduced by **à** is an idea, and this too is referred back to by **y**.

Note that *there* can often be left out in English, but **y** can <u>never</u> be omitted in French.

Je vais. ✗
J'y vais. ✓ — *I'm going.*

Tu penses <u>à cette recette de cuisine</u> ?	*Are you thinking about that recipe?*
Oui, j'<u>y</u> pense.	*Yes, I'm thinking about <u>it</u>.*

HOW TO USE 'EN'

En replaces **du, de la, de l', des** + noun (**du poivre, de la farine, de l'eau, des œufs**) or a definite quantity of something; for example, **cent grammes de...** (*one hundred grammes of...*), **dix mètres de...** (ten metres of...), **un paquet de...** (*a packet of...*).

En is the equivalent in English of *some* or *any*.

Vous voulez <u>des tomates</u> ?	*Do you want some tomatoes?*
Vous <u>en</u> voulez ?	*Do you want <u>some</u>?*

In a sentence with **beaucoup de** (*a lot of*), **peu de** (*a little of*), **assez de** (*enough of*), **trop de** (*too much of*) or a number plus noun (**trois kilos de..., cinq mètres de..., deux litres de..., un paquet de...**), **en** replaces the noun and the quantity. The number, or the word **beaucoup, peu** or **assez**, for example, is then placed at the end of the sentence.

Il y a <u>beaucoup de chambres</u>.	*There are a lot of rooms.*
Il y a beaucoup d'elles. ✕	
Il y <u>en</u> a <u>beaucoup</u>. ✓	*There are a lot (of them).*
Je voudrais <u>deux livres</u>.	*I'd like two books.*
Je voudrais deux. ✕	
J'<u>en</u> voudrais <u>deux</u>. ✓	*I'd like two (of them).*

En can also mean *from there* when talking about a place, or *about it*:

Connaissez-vous Paris ?	*Do you know Paris?*
Oui, je viens de Paris.	*Yes, I come from Paris.*
Oui, j'<u>en</u> viens.	*Yes, I come from there.*
Il parle de son enfance.	*He talks about his childhood.*
Il <u>en</u> parle.	*He talks about it.*

16 Reflect on your reflexives!

WHAT IS A REFLEXIVE VERB?

Let's look first of all at what a reflexive verb is. All verbs are words which describe an action. Often the action (e.g. washing) is performed on something, or someone else:

Je lave la voiture.	*I wash the car.*
Marie habille sa sœur.	*Marie is dressing her sister.*

However, when the verb involves nothing or nobody else, in French you slip an extra matching pronoun between the actor and the verb, i.e the action 'reflects back' on the subject, like the things we do in front of the mirror.

Je <u>me</u> lave.	*I am washing myself/having a wash/ getting washed.*
Tu <u>te</u> rases.	*You are shaving (yourself).*
Elle <u>se</u> regarde.	*She is looking at herself.*
Nous <u>nous</u> douchons.	*We are having a shower.*
Vous <u>vous</u> habillez.	*You are dressing (yourself/yourselves)/ getting dressed.*
Ils <u>se</u> couchent.	*They are going to bed.*

These verbs are usually taught in lessons which involve daily routines and we learn them by heart. They include **s'habiller** (*to get dressed*), **se réveiller** (*to wake up*), **se lever** (*to get up*), **se laver** (*to get washed*) and **se doucher** (*to have a shower*).

USING REFLEXIVE PRONOUNS: 'ME', 'TE', 'SE', 'NOUS' AND 'VOUS'

The problem comes when reflexive verbs become so fixed in the mind in the **se réveiller** or **se lever** form that the **se** becomes firmly attached. However, often a change of pronoun is needed; for example, after the words **pour** (*in order to*), **pouvoir** (*to be able*) and **préférer** (*to prefer*).

Je me couche tôt pour se réveiller tôt. ✗	
Je me couche tôt pour <u>me</u> réveiller tôt. ✓	*I am going to bed early so as to get up early.*
Tu ne veux pas se lever. ✗	
<u>**Tu**</u> **ne veux pas <u>te</u> lever.** ✓	*You don't want to get up.*
Vous pouvez s'habiller maintenant. ✗	
<u>**Vous**</u> **pouvez <u>vous</u> habiller maintenant.** ✓	*You can get dressed now.*

Instead, there must always be a match between the lead actor (**je, tu,** etc.) and the pronoun (**me, te,** etc.). Here are the matching pairs:

je	**me**
tu	**te**
il(elle)(on)	**se**
nous	**nous**
vous	**vous**
ils(elles)	**se**

Insight

In French we know who the parts of the body belong to because of the use of the reflexive pronoun **me,** so you don't have to say it again by using the possessive adjectives **mon/ ma/mes** (*my*), etc.!

<u>**Je me**</u> **lave <u>les</u> cheveux, <u>le</u> visage et <u>les</u> mains.** ✓	*I am washing my hair, my face and my hands.*

17a Disjunctive and emphatic pronouns: **moi, toi, lui, elle, nous, vous, eux** and **elles**

PRONOUNS IN GREETINGS

Strong (or disjunctive) pronouns are commonly used in greetings:

Ça va ? Très bien merci et <u>toi</u> ?   *How are you? Very well thank you and <u>you</u>?*

Chez <u>moi</u> ou chez <u>toi</u> ?   *At <u>my house</u> or at <u>yours</u>?*

PRONOUNS FOR EMPHASIS

The pronouns **moi, toi, lui, elle, nous, vous, eux** and **elles** are also used to express an opinion or to help make a point in a conversation or an argument. In English we stress the equivalent word *I*, or *he*, for example, to produce the same effect.

<u>Moi, je</u> pense qu'il a raison.   *In <u>my</u> opinion, he is right.*

<u>Moi</u>, par contre, <u>je</u> pense qu'il a tort.   *<u>I</u>, on the other hand, think he is wrong.*

<u>Lui, il</u> pense que la récession est finie.   *<u>He</u> thinks that the recession is over.*

<u>Nous, nous</u> n'aimons pas aller au cinéma.   *<u>We</u> do not like going to the cinema.*

<u>Eux, ils</u> sont toujours en retard.   *<u>They</u> are always late.*

Disjunctive pronouns are also used when there are multiple subjects separated by a comma, **et** (*and*) or **ou** (*or*) to distinguish between one person and the other.

Qui commence ? <u>Toi</u> ou <u>moi</u> ?   *Who starts? <u>You</u> or <u>me</u>?*

Demandez-<u>lui</u> !   *Ask <u>him</u>!*

À qui ? À <u>elle</u> ou à <u>lui</u> ?   *Ask who? <u>Him</u> or <u>her</u>?*

Même is often added to the disjunctive pronouns to give **moi-même** (*myself*), **toi-même** (*yourself*), **elle-même** (*herself*), **lui-même**

(*himself*), **soi-même** (*oneself*), **nous-mêmes** (*ourselves*), **vous-même** (*yourself*, formal), **vous-mêmes** (*yourselves*) and **eux-mêmes** (*themselves*, m.pl.) and **elles-mêmes** (*themselves*, f.pl.). This is very useful when speaking on the phone:

«Je voudrais parler à Monsieur Jacques Dupont, s'il vous plaît !	*"Could I speak to Mr Jacques Dupont, please?"*
— Lui-même ! »	*"Speaking!"*
« Mademoiselle Prion est là ?	*"Is Miss Prion there?"*
— Elle-même ! »	*"Speaking!"*

'SOI' *ONE* AND 'SOI-MÊME' *ONESELF*

Soi should be used when no particular person is intended, as is the case with the pronoun **on** (*one, you, we* or *people* in a general sense) (see Chapter 50) and the phrases **il faut** (*it is essential to…, one must…*) and **c'est bien/mal de** (*it is good/bad to…*).

C'est bien de rentrer chez <u>soi</u> après des vacances.	*It is lovely to be back home after a holiday.* (i.e. not in your home or my home, but more generally 'in one's home')
On l'a fait <u>soi-même</u>.	*We did it <u>ourselves</u>.* (i.e. each person, in general, did it themselves)

But do not use **soi-même** when a particular person <u>is</u>, or persons <u>are</u>, intended. Look at the following examples:

Il conduit <u>lui-même</u> pour aller au bureau.	*He drives <u>himself</u> to work.*
Elle a fait ce gâteau <u>elle-même</u>.	*She made the cake <u>herself</u>.*
Pierre et George veulent le faire <u>eux-mêmes</u>.	*Pierre and Georges want to do it <u>themselves</u>.*

Insight

Using emphatic pronouns will make you sound so French! Just listen to well-known politicians talking on the radio or TV – you will now notice how often they are used!

17b His or hers, mine or yours? Possessive adjectives and pronouns

OWNERSHIP – IS IT 'HIS' OR 'HER' BROTHER?

Here are a few typical mistakes made by learners:

Voici il frère. ✗
Voici elle frère. ✗
Voici sa frère. ✗
Voici <u>son</u> frère. ✓   *Here is his/her brother.*
C'est elle sœur ? ✗
C'est il sœur ? ✗
C'est <u>sa</u> sœur ? ✓   *Is it her/his sister?*

The word **son** (*his, her*) is used in place of the masculine words
un (*a*) or **le** (*the*); and **sa** (*his, her*) is used in place of the feminine
words **une** (*a*) or **la** (*the*). So, **son** and **sa** indicate to whom or to what
they belong. These possessive adjectives are used in a similar way
as the English *his* and *her*, but there are fundamental differences as
you can see from the English translation of these examples.

Whereas in English we have only *my, your, his, her, our* and *their*
to choose between, French is more complicated:

1 Use **mon/ma** (*my*), **ton/ta** (*your,* familiar), **son/sa** (*his/her*),
   notre (*our*), **votre** (*your,* formal and plural) and **leur** (*their*)
   when there is one possession, i.e. the thing possessed is in the
   singular.
2 Use **mes** (*my*), **tes** (*your*), **ses** (*his/hers*), **nos** (*our*), **vos** (*your*)
   and **leurs** (*their*) when there is more than one possession,
   i.e. the thing possessed is in its plural form.
3 In contrast with English, whether the owner of the object is
   female or male is of no consequence whatsoever. It is only the
   gender (**un** or **une**) and quantity of the thing possessed that
   matters.
   So, **une voiture** (*a car*) becomes **sa voiture** (*his/her car*) or <u>**ses**</u>
   voiture<u>s</u> (*his/her cars*) regardless of the gender of the owner.

You can see how important it is to know whether a word is masculine (**un/le**) or feminine (**une/la**)!

4 When the noun begins with a vowel ('a', 'e', 'i', 'o' and 'u'), there is a change from **ma** to **mon**, from **ta** to **ton** and from **sa** to **son** for reasons of flow and ease of pronunciation despite the gender of the noun. So, **une amie** (*a friend*) should become '**ma amie**' (*my friend*), but it does not. For ease of pronunciation, we instead say <u>**mon**</u> **amie** (*my (girl) friend*).

IS IT MINE OR YOURS? POSSESSIVE PRONOUNS

Here, French and English are very similar in usage. However, in French we have to remember the agreements in number and gender. Either **le**, **la**, or **les** <u>must</u> precede **mien(ne)(s)**, **tien(ne)(s)**, **sien(ne)(s)**, **nôtre(s)**, **vôtre(s)** and **leur(s)**. So:

le mien, la mienne, les miens, les miennes	*mine*
le tien, la tienne, les tiens, les tiennes	*yours* (familiar)
le sien, la sienne, les siens, les siennes	*his/hers*
le nôtre, la nôtre, les nôtres	*ours*
le vôtre, la vôtre, les vôtres	*yours* (formal, plural)
le leur, la leur, les leurs	*theirs*

Now consider the following examples:

Je vois ton frère, mais <u>le mien</u> n'est pas encore arrivé. ✓	*I can see your brother (<u>**un** frère</u>), but <u>mine</u> hasn't arrived yet.*
Je déteste ma voiture ; <u>la tienne</u> est beaucoup plus jolie. ✓	*I hate my car (<u>**une** voiture</u>); <u>yours</u> is much better looking.*

Insight

Notice that in the above sentence the 'e' at the end of **joli<u>e</u>** agrees with <u>**la tienne**</u>.

18a Gender issues – very French!

Do you go to **la poste** or **le poste** to post a letter? In French, it is almost impossible to talk about an object or a concept without its attached article – either definite (**le/ la/ l'/ les**) or indefinite (**un/une/des**) – or a number and a quantity (e.g. **deux kilos, cinq livres**). (See Chapter 19a.)

Every noun (a thing, physical or abstract, or a person) is either preceded by:

▶ **un** (*one*), **une** (*one*) or **des** (*some*): **une tasse** (*a cup*), **une table** (*a table*), **un verre** (*a glass*), **un sac** (*a bag*), **une liberté** (*a freedom*), **une idée** (*an idea*), **des projets** (*some plans*), **un homme** (*a man*), **une femme** (*a woman*), **des chiens** (*some dogs*), **un vieillard** (*an old man*); or

▶ **le** (*the*), **la** (*the*), **l'** (*the*) and **les** (*the*) for things and concepts which are universally shared: **le Pakistan** (*Pakistan*), **la liberté** (*freedom*), **l'océan Pacifique** (*the Pacific Ocean*), **les Français** (*the French*).

Objects which have been already been referred to in a conversation become the pronouns **le, la, l'** and **les** respectively. (See Chapters 13a, 13b.)

You can see this illustrated in the following dialogue.

« Où est **le livre** de Pierre ? Je ne **le** trouve pas.	"Where is Pierre's book? I cannot find it."
— Il est sur **la table** dans la cuisine. Tu **la** vois ? Près **des fenêtres** qui donnent sur le jardin.	"It is on the table in the kitchen. Can you see it? By the windows overlooking the garden."
— Ah oui, je **les** vois, merci. »	"Thank you, I can see them."

Sous la Porsche, ou sous le porche ?

IT'S IMPORTANT TO GET THE GENDER OF A NOUN RIGHT!

Getting the gender of a word wrong can be very misleading, as in the following cases which, depending on whether they are given a masculine or feminine article, will mean very different things!

Do you go to **un poste** (*a position* or *a job*) or **une poste** (*a post office*) to post a letter? It matters!

Do you have **un livre** (*a book*) or **une livre** (*a pound*)?

Is it **un manche** (*a handle*), **une manche** (*a sleeve*) or **la Manche** (*the Channel*)?

Do you want to experience **un tour** (*a turn, trick* or *walk about*) or see **une tour** (*a tower*)?

Is it **un voile** (*a veil*) or **une voile** (*a sail*) that you wear on your head?

18b Which nouns are masculine and which are feminine?

HOW CAN YOU TELL IF A NOUN IS MASCULINE OR FEMININE?

Now, how can one predict whether a word is going to be masculine (**un**) or feminine (**une**) without memorizing each word individually? Native speakers do not simply rely on their memory – they generally recognize patterns which determine whether a noun is masculine or feminine, which makes it much simpler. All they then need to do is to remember the exceptions! Look at the following lists and notice the patterns in the word endings which can help us to predict whether a word is masculine or feminine.

▶ The following groups of words tend to be masculine:

1 Words ending in '-c', '-u', '-n', '-i' and '-t' tend to be **un** words: **un sac** (*bag*), **un tableau** (*painting*), **un garçon** (*a boy*), **un ami** (*a friend*), **un chat** (*a cat*).

2 Words ending in '-asme' tend to be **un** words: **un enthusiasme**, **un sarcasme**.

3 Words ending in '-é' are often **un** words: **un thé** (*a tea*), **un café** (*a café* or *a coffee*), **un supermarché** (*a supermarket*), **un dé** (*a die*).

4 Words ending '-age' are usually **un** words: **un âge** (*an age*), **un mariage** (*a marriage*), **un visage** (*a face*), **un paysage** (*a landscape*). Remember the main exceptions in this group: **la plage** (*beach*) which you capture in **une image** (*picture*) which you stick onto **une page** (*page*)!

5 Words ending in '-aire' tend to be **un** words: **un commissaire** (*a police superintendant*), **un vestiaire** (*a cloakroom*), **un corsaire** (*a pirate*).

6 Words ending in '-ème' are usually **un** words: **un poème** (*a poem*), **un système** (*a system*), **un thème** (*a theme, a translation*).

7 Words ending in '-ice' are usually **un** words: **un dentifrice**
(*a toothpaste*), **un sacrifice** (*a sacrifice*), **un service** (*a service*).

▶ The following groups of words tend to be feminine:

8 Words ending in '-e' are often **une** words: **une salle** (*a room*), **une voiture** (*a car*), **une boutique** (*a shop*), **une table** (*a table*).

9 Words ending in '-ion' are often **une** words: **une version**
(*a version* or *a translation*), **une nation** (*a nation*), **une profession**
(*a profession*), **une situation** (*a situation*).

10 Words ending in '-té' (usually ideas or concepts) are often
une words: **une liberté** (*a freedom*), **une égalité** (*an equality*), **une modalité** (*a form* or *a mode*).

Of course, French would not be a challenge if there were no
exceptions! Look at the genders of the following nouns:

un théâtre	*a theatre*
un lycée	*a secondary school (15–18 years)*
un collège	*a secondary school (10–15 years)*
un centre	*a centre*

And don't forget that many words can be **un** or **une** depending on
whether the person you're referring to is male or female, without
it affecting the spelling of the word, e.g. **un/une adulte** (*adult*),
un/une célibataire (*single person*), **un/une collègue** (*colleague*),
un/une dentiste (*dentist*), **un/une élève** (*pupil*), **un/une enfant**
(*child*), **un/une fonctionnaire** (*civil servant*), **un/une journaliste**
(*journalist*), **un/une pensionnaire** (*boarder*), **un/une photographe**
(*photographer*), **un/une professeur** (*teacher*).

Insight

Although it is important to get the gender of nouns right,
especially where there is a possible slip of meaning, do not
worry too much about the occasional mistake. What is
important is to be consistent and to get your meaning across
to your listener.

19a Be articulate! The indefinite, definite and partitive articles

CHOOSING BETWEEN 'UN'/'UNE' AND 'LE'/'LA'/'LES'

'Un' and 'une'

Using the indefinite articles **un** and **une** (*a, an*) is pretty straightforward: wherever you would say *a* or *an* in English, in French you use **un** or **une**, depending on whether the word that follows is masculine or feminine.

Philippe aime bien prendre <u>un</u> verre le soir au bar.	*Philippe likes going to the pub for <u>a</u> drink in the evening.*
Il prend toujours <u>une</u> limonade.	*He always has <u>a</u> lemonade.*

'Le', 'la' and 'les'

The definite articles **le**, **la** and **les** (*the*, masculine, feminine and plural) replace the English word *the*.

<u>Le</u> pub est comfortable et <u>la</u> serveuse lui plaît.	*<u>The</u> pub is cosy and he fancies <u>the</u> barmaid.*

Le and **la** are abbreviated to **l'** before a vowel and mute 'h'.

<u>L'</u>eau minérale est sur la table.	*<u>The</u> mineral water is on the table.*
<u>L'</u>hôtel est trop loin de la gare.	*<u>The</u> hotel is too far from the station.*

However, even where you can do without the words *a, an* or *the* in English, the use of **un** and **une**, or **le, la, l'** and **les** is absolutely essential in French.

J'aime bière, mais vin est bon aussi. ✗	*I like beer but wine is nice too.*
J'aime <u>la</u> bière mais <u>le</u> vin est bon aussi. ✓	*I like beer but wine is nice too.*

In the first example, the words **bière** and **vin** do not make sense in French on their own; part of their identity is missing and your listener or reader expects more. Where you're making a general, non-specific statement, use **le**, **la** or **les**.

<u>Les</u> cocktails ne sont pas pour moi, et <u>l'</u>eau est dégoûtante.	*Cocktails are not for me, and water is horrible.*
<u>Les</u> Français aiment bien <u>les</u> pubs anglais.	*French people like English pubs.*
<u>La</u> vie est belle.	*Life is good.*

'DU', 'DE LA', 'DE L'' AND 'DES' *SOME*

Use **du**, **de la**, **de l'** and **des** to refer to a vague quantity of something, or when in English the word *some* could comfortably be slipped in front of the nouns in the sentence (even if in English we would normally leave it out).

Hier soir j'ai bu <u>du</u> vin, <u>de la</u> bière, <u>des</u> cocktails et même <u>de l'</u>eau.	*Yesterday evening I drank (some) wine, (some) beer, (some) cocktails and even (some) water.*

Insight

After a negative, when in English we would often use the word *any*, **du**, **de la**, **de l'** and **des** all change to **de** or **d'**.

Ce soir je n'ai pas bu <u>d'</u>alcool.	*This evening I didn't drink <u>any</u> alcohol.*

19b When to use **un/une** and **le/la/les** with days or parts of a day

DAYS OF THE WEEK

Is it happening on Monday, does it generally happen on Mondays or did it happen on one particular Monday? When it comes to days of the week, it is important to be specific in order to distinguish between one occurrence, a habitual occurrence and a specific event in the past.

Lundi, elle va à la piscine.	*On Monday, she is going swimming.*
Le lundi/Les lundis, je vais à la piscine.	*On Mondays I go swimming.*
Un lundi, j'étais au travail quand le téléphone a sonné. C'était le président des États-Unis !	*One Monday, I was at work when the phone rang. It was the president of the United States!*

PARTS OF THE DAY

A day is divided up into:

le matin	*the morning*
l'après-midi	*the afternoon*
le soir	*the evening*
la nuit	*the night*

To describe <u>when</u> you do something, the above are the terms to use, with no extra words added. Don't be tempted to add à or dans, even if it feels odd.

Le matin, je pars à mon travail.	*In the morning I go to work.*
Je rentre tard **le soir**.	*I get home late in the evenings.*
La nuit, je fais la fête !	*At night, I go out and have fun!*

If, however, you are describing an activity which occupied one of those periods of time, some different words may need to be used:

la matinée	*the morning*
la soirée	*the evening*

J'ai passé le soir à lire. ✗	
J'ai passé la soirée à lire. ✓	*I spent the evening reading.*
Pendant la matinée j'ai fait mes devoirs.	*During the morning I did my homework.*

PAST AND FUTURE

When you are talking about one particular day, or part of a day, in the past or in the future **un/une** are the words to use before **matinée** (*morning*), **après-midi** (*afternoon*), **soirée** (*evening*) and **la nuit** (*night*), again depending on whether you are just talking about the time something happened, or something to which you devoted that time. Look at the following examples:

J'ai passé toute <u>une matinée</u> à flâner dans les rues.	*I spent a whole morning wandering round the streets.*
Un jour, je ne suis pas allé au bureau.	*One day I didn't go into the office.*
J'ai passé <u>une journée</u> à faire les magasins.	*I spent a (whole) day shopping.*
Demain, je vais passer <u>la soirée</u> chez mes amis.	*Tomorrow, I'm going to spend the evening with my friends.*

....

Insight

Use the preposition **à** as part of a farewell to someone when you are expecting to see them some time in the future; e.g. **À mardi !** (*Till Tuesday, then!*), **À la semaine prochaine !** (*See you next week!*), **À plus !** (with the 's' of **plus** pronounced) (*See you later!*)

....

20 Agreement of adjectives – the French all agree on this!

Adjectives (*good, bad, ugly*) supply information about people, situations and things. In English, no matter whether you describe someone's clothes, their house, their wife or their manners, the adjective remains the same. It's a nice, neat arrangement.

NOUNS AND ADJECTIVES IN FRENCH MUST AGREE!

In French the spelling of the adjective, as well as where it is placed, will be influenced by the choice of adjective and what it is describing. Most adjectives in French are placed <u>after</u> the word they are describing:

Regarde le pull bleu ! ✓　　　　　*Look at the blue pullover!*

But there's another important difference. The adjective ending has to match the gender of the word it is describing:

Regarde la robe verte ! ✓　　　　*Look at the green dress!*

The ending of the adjective **vert** (*green*) has to be changed to match the gender of **la robe** (*dress*); here an extra 'e' has to be added to the end of the adjective. In this example, this also changes the sound. When you add the extra 'e' to the end of **vert**, the 't' is pronounced, whereas before it was silent.

Ces vêtements sont élégant. ✗
Ces vêtements sont élégants. ✓　　　*These clothes are stylish.*

You can see that an 's' has been added to the end of **élégant** to match the plural noun **vêtements**. Where the noun being described is feminine and plural, an extra 'es' must be added to the end of the adjective.

<u>**Les chemisiers**</u> **verts sont jolis, et**　　　*The green blouses are nice, and*
　<u>**les robes**</u> **grises sont jolies aussi.**　　*the grey dresses are nice too.*

When an adjective already ends in '-e' (e.g. **rose**, *pink*) or '-s' (e.g. **gris**, *grey*), leave well alone:

Mon amie préfère la jupe rose et les pulls gris.

My friend prefers the pink skirt and grey jumpers.

IRREGULAR ADJECTIVES

Some adjectives do not follow the rules just described; they are irregular. Changes from the masculine to feminine ending occur and these changes just have to be learned. Some of the most common of these irregular adjectives fit into categories, and it may be helpful to identify patterns:

Singular			Plural	
masculine	feminine		masculine	feminine
Doubling the final letter				
mignon	**mignonne**	*(cute)*	**mignons**	**mignonnes**
gros	**grosse**	*(fat)*	**gros**	**grosses**
gentil	**gentille**	*(kind)*	**gentils**	**gentilles**
ancien	**ancienne**	*(ancient, former)*	**anciens**	**anciennes**
Changing the ending				
délicieux	**délicieuse**	*(tasty)*	**délicieux**	**délicieuses**
sportif	**sportive**	*(sporty)*	**sportifs**	**sportives**
fou	**folle**	*(mad)*	**fous**	**folles**
Some are completely irregular				
beau	**belle**	*(handsome, beautiful)*	**beaux**	**belles**
long	**longue**	*(long)*	**longs**	**longues**
frais	**fraîche**	*(fresh)*	**frais**	**fraîches**
faux	**fausse**	*(false)*	**faux**	**fausses**

Just a few, mostly colours, never change!

marron, châtain *(chestnut brown)*

bleu-marine *(navy blue)*

21a How you do what you do: **bon**, **bien**, **mauvais** and **mal**

'LE VIN EST BON !'

Good, *bad*, *well* and *badly* cause many problems with learners, as the following common error shows.

Vous aimez ce vin ?	*Do you like this wine?*
Oui, il est bien. ✗	
Oui, il est bon. ✓	*Yes, it is good.*

A wine cannot be **bien** (*well*)! A wine can either be **bon** (*good*) or **mauvais** (*bad*). If you wish to compliment someone on their cooking, use **C'est bon !** (*It's good! It tastes good!*) Avoid **C'est bien** if you want to respond positively to an artistic performance or creation.

Tu as aimé le film ? Oui, c'était bon.	*Did you like the film? Yes, it was good.*
La peinture/le paysage/le coucher du soleil est beau/ magnifique.	*The painting/landscape/sunset is beautiful/superb.*

Bon and **mauvais** are adjectives – they are usually used to describe nouns. They may also be used to describe physical sensations or feelings: **C'est bon de vous revoir !** (*It is good to see you again!*)

Bon and **mauvais** are also used to describe the weather for the same reason: **Il fait bon** (*It is warm*). One can almost feel the pleasure of the warmth...

Mauvais is the opposite of **bon**: **Il fait mauvais** (*The weather is terrible*). And while the weather is terrible, we feel the same...

'JE VAIS BIEN, MERCI, ET VOUS/TOI ?' I'M WELL, THANKS, AND YOU?

Bien and **mal** are adverbs. They are mostly used to describe intellectual, judgemental, moral or ethical qualities of somebody or something's actions. They offer a subjective appraisal. For example, a teacher could say of a good piece of writing: **C'est bien (fait)** ! (*It is good!* or *It is well done!*); **C'est bien (écrit)** ! (*It is good!* or *It is well written!*); or **C'est bon** ! (i.e. reading it gave me a lot of pleasure).

Only when **bien** and **mal** follow the action they evaluate can they actually suggest how well or badly something is done:

Patricia conduit bien.	*Patricia drives well.*
Pierre parle mal grec.	*Pierre speaks Greek badly.*

Bien and **mal** are useful if you need to say that you don't understand something well, or if you wish to ask for clarification:

J'ai mal compris, je vous prie de m'excuser.	*I didn't understand, please forgive me.*
Est-ce que j'ai bien compris, vous m'avez demandé l'heure ?	*Have I understood this correctly, you asked me the time?*

Votre Majestée, le peuple n'a plus de pain et meurt de faim !
(Your Majesty, the people have no bread left and are dying of hunger!)

Hé bien, mon brave, qu'ils mangent donc du gâteau, c'est bien meilleur !
(Well, then, my good man, let them eat cake, it's much better!)

21b Making comparisons

FOR BETTER OR FOR WORSE

In French, it's easy to compare one thing with another – use **plus** (*more*), **moins** (*less*) and **aussi** (*as*) before the adjective, and **que** (*than*) before the thing you are comparing it with:

Le pain est plus frais que les gâteaux.	*The bread is fresher than the cakes.*
Le pain est aussi frais que les gâteaux.	*The bread is as fresh as the cakes.*

But you must remember to make the adjective agree with the noun in the usual way (see Chapter 20).

<u>**Cette baguette**</u> **est moins** <u>**fraîche**</u> **que l'autre.**	*This French stick is less fresh than the other one.*
<u>**Les gâteaux**</u> **sont plus chers que le pain.**	*The cakes are more expensive than the bread.*

Use **meilleur (que)** (*better (than)*) to compare things. Don't forget to make the adjective agree!

Les gâteaux sont meilleurs que les croissants.	*The cakes are better than the croissants.*

Pire (*worse*) compares two things which are already bad, but is usually only used in set expressions, e.g. **Le remède est pire que le mal !** (*The cure is worse than the illness!*)

To compare actions, use **aussi bien que** (*as well as*), **aussi mal que** (*as badly as*), **mieux (que)** (*better (than)*) and **moins bien que** (*less well than*). Because they're adverbs, they don't agree.

Pierre chante aussi bien/mal que toi.	*Pierre sings as well/badly as you.*

THE MOST AND THE LEAST

If you want to describe something as 'the ...est' (e.g. *the tallest, the most/least interesting*, i.e. the superlative), use **le plus/le moins** with masculine singular adjectives, **la plus/la moins** with feminine singular adjectives and **les plus** with plural adjectives. Watch out for word order:

C'est la région la moins   *It's the least interesting region*
intéressante de France.   *of France.*

If the adjective usually goes after the noun, then the superlative goes after the noun too, but if the adjective usually goes before the noun, then the superlative will do so as well:

C'est un haut monument. C'est le   *It's a tall building. It's the tallest*
plus haut monument de Paris.   *building in Paris.*

In superlative sentences, *in* is **de**, not **dans**, e.g. **Le membre le plus adroit <u>de</u> l'équipe** (*The most skilful member in the team*).

THE BEST AND THE WORST

Use **le/la/les meilleur(s)** for *the best*, **le/la/les pire(s)** for *the worst*:

C'est le meilleur film de l'année.   *It's the best film of the year.*
<u>La</u> cuisine italienne est <u>la</u>   *Italian food is the best in*
<u>meilleure</u> du monde.   *the world.*

Comparative and superlative adjectives can also be used with adverbs, e.g. **Ce sont les Anglais qui boivent le plus de thé** (*The English drink the most tea*).

··
Insight
Pis (*worse*) and le pis (*worst*) occur only in fixed expressions:

Tant pis !	*Never mind!*
Les choses vont de pis en pis/	*Things are going from bad to*
de mal en pis.	*worse.*
Qui pis est...	*What is worse...*
··

22a Tout, toutes, tous or toutes?

Tout (*all*) and its variant forms have several meanings in French and they are not much liked by learners who are often uncertain as to how to use them as well as how to pronounce them.

1 Tout le..., tous les..., toute la..., toutes les... (*all the*) as adjectives:

As we know, all adjectives must agree with the noun they are describing (see Chapter 20), and this includes **tout** which must reflect the gender and number of the thing it precedes. In front of a masculine singular noun, use **tout le**; before a masculine plural noun use **tous les**; before a feminine singular noun, use **toute la**; and before a feminine plural noun, use **toutes les**:

<u>Tout le pays</u> aime la femme du président.	*The whole country like the president's wife.*
<u>Tous les gouvernements</u> font des chapters.	*All governments make mistakes.*
<u>Toute la planète</u> est en danger.	*The whole planet is in danger.*
<u>Toutes les femmes</u> aiment la couleur rose.	*All women like the colour pink.*

In the above examples the 't' is only heard when followed by 'e', e.g. **toute**. The 's' of **tous** is always silent when followed by **les**, e.g. **Tous les hommes du président** (*All the president's men*).

2 Tout as a pronoun:

▶ tout (*everything, all*) may be used to replace an abstract noun. Here, **tout** has no gender since it is not associated with a particular word; used in this way, **tout** always has a silent 't'.

C'est tout !	*That is all!*
Tout est perdu !	*All is lost!*
Tout va bien !	*All is well!*

▶ **tous/toutes** (*all*) may be used as pronouns in reference to people or animals. As a pronoun, the 's' of **tous** is always sounded.

Nous sommes tous ici.	*We are all here.*
Ils sont tous morts.	*They all died.*
Mes enfants, ils aiment tous les bonbons.	*My children all like sweets.* (Here, **tous** is the pronoun replacing **mes enfants**.)
Elles ont toutes vingt ans.	*They are all twenty.*

3 Tout (*completely, very*) as an adverb:

Il parle tout bas.	*He talks very quietly.*
Nous habitons tout près d'ici.	*We live nearby.*
C'est tout simple.	*It's very easy.*

4 Tout is used in everyday set expressions, especially in the following contexts. When followed by a vowel, the 't' of **tout** is sounded.

▶ time;

| À tout à l'heure ! | *See you later!* |
| À tout de suite ! | *See you in a moment!* |

▶ when shopping and talking about money;

| Cela fait 100 euros en tout. | *That comes to 100 euros in all/in total.* |
| C'est tout neuf. | *It's brand new.* |

▶ when giving an opinion.

| Tout à fait ! | *Absolutely!* |
| C'est de toute beauté ! | *It's extremely beautiful!* |

22b How to pronounce **tous**, and using **tous les/toutes les**

Tous pour un et un pour tous !
(All for one and one for all !)

WHEN SHOULD I PRONOUNCE THE 'S' IN 'TOUS'?

This is a frequently asked question. Sometimes you hear the 's' in tous, and sometimes you do not.

Richard regarde tous (sounding the 's') **les sports à la télévision.** ✗
Richard regarde tous (with a silent 's') **les sports à la télévision.** ✓   *Richard watches every sport on television.*

Here are two simple rules to help you avoid this easy mistake:

1 When **tous** is an adjective (see Chapter 22a), the 's' is silent. Tous with a silent 's' is always followed by **les**:
Tous les enfants aiment les animaux.   *All children like animals.*

2 When **tous** is a pronoun (see Chapter 22a), the 's' is heard :
Mes enfants, ils aiment tous les animaux.   *My children all like animals.*
(Here, **tous** is a pronoun replacing 'all my children'.)

Be careful! While both the following sentences are correct, they have very different meanings depending on whether the 's' is pronounced or not:

Ils regardent tous (with a silent 's') **les sports à la télévision.**
They watch <u>all the sports</u> on television.

Ils regardent tous (sounding the 's') **les sports à la télévision.**
They <u>all</u> watch sport on the television.

'TOUS LES' AND 'TOUTES LES' TO EXPRESS FREQUENCY

Tous les (*every*, before a masculine plural noun) and **toutes les** (*every*, before a feminine plural noun) can be used to talk about how often something happens.

tous les jours	*every day*
tous les deux jours	*every other day*
tous les mois	*every month*
Je vais au marché toutes les deux semaines.	*I go to the market every two weeks.*
Il voit ses collègues tous les jeudis.	*He sees his colleagues every Thursday.*

Insight

When a feminine adjective starts with a vowel, e.g. **excitée** (*excited*), or a silent 'h', e.g. **heureuse** (*happy*), the agreement of **tout** with thing/person it is describing is optional:

Elle est toute/tout excitée de le revoir.
She is thoroughly excited to see him again.

Vous étiez toute/tout heureuse de participer à l'émission.
You were delighted to go on the programme.

Elle était toute/tout élégante.
She was really elegant.

Used in this way, **tout/toute** gives additional emphasis to the adjective.

23 C'est and il/elle est... Defining moments

'IL EST' OR 'ELLE EST'?

The neuter word *it* in English refers to a genderless, inanimate object or notion. However, as we know, in French every object, notion or idea has a gender. So, *it* in French – when it is the subject of a sentence – has to be either the masculine **il** or the feminine **elle**. (See Chapters 13a and 13b for 'it' as a direct object pronoun.)

J'ai acheté <u>le livre</u> (m.) <u>Il</u> est ici.	I bought <u>the book</u>. <u>It</u> is here.
<u>La fin</u> (f.) était intéressante.	<u>The end</u> was interesting.
<u>Elle</u> m'a surpris.	<u>It</u> surprised me.

In some situations, however, the word **ce** is used where we would say *it* in English.

SHOULD I USE 'C'EST' OR 'IL/ELLE EST' BEFORE AN ADJECTIVE?

This is tricky. As a general rule, use **il/elle est** before an adjective in reference to a thing or person, but use **c'est** when referring to a general idea, an abstract noun, a system or an impression.

J'aime bien ce roman. <u>Il</u> est très original.	I really like that novel. <u>It</u>'s very original.
Ta copine, elle est belle !	Your girl friend is beautiful!
J'aime beaucoup lire en vacances. <u>C'est</u> formidable !	I really like reading on holiday. <u>It</u>'s great!

Il est ... de is used when the adjective refers forward to something about to be mentioned, and **c'est** is used to refer back to something already mentioned.

Il est impossible de faire une réservation.	It's impossible to make a reservation.
C'est impossible ?	Is it impossible?
Il est intéressant d'écouter les actualités.	It's interesting to listen to the news.
Oui, c'est même essentiel.	Yes, it's essential.

'C'EST' IS USED BEFORE A NOUN AND AS A DEFINITION

Ce is always used before the verb être when this is followed directly by **un/une, le/la**, by a possessive adjective or by a name.

Dans ce roman <u>c'est Jérôme</u> qui découvre que <u>c'est le</u> père de la fille qui est le coupable. <u>C'est une</u> honte.

Qu'est-ce que <u>c'est</u> ?

<u>C'est</u>/voici/voilà <u>un</u> crime passionnel !

In this novel <u>it is</u> Jérôme who discovers that <u>it is</u> the father of the girl who is the guilty one. <u>It's</u> shameful.

What is it?

It's a crime of passion!

'C'EST' IS USED BEFORE A STRONG PRONOUN

C'est is used to translate *it is* when followed by an emphatic pronoun: **moi** (*me*), **toi** (*you*, familiar), **lui** (*him*), **elle** (*her*), **nous** (*we*), **vous** (*you*, polite), **eux/elles** (*them*, m. pl., f. pl.).

<u>C'est lui</u>, et <u>ce</u> n'<u>est</u> pas <u>elle</u>.

It's him and not her

24 You're never alone with a plural!

In most cases the plural of a noun is formed by adding an 's' to the singular, just like in English, although in French you do not usually hear this final 's'.

un étudiant   *a student*   **des étudiants**   *(some) students*

As in English there are some exceptions to this plural rule.

IRREGULAR PLURAL ENDINGS

▶ Words ending in -**al**, -**eu** and -**eau** add an 'x' in the plural.

Singular	Plural	
un cheval	**des chevaux**	*horses*
un cheveu	**des cheveux**	*hair(s)*
un tableau	**des tableaux**	*pictures*

There are a few exceptions; here are two useful ones:

un festival	**des festivals**	*festivals*
un pneu	**des pneus**	*tyres*

▶ Words ending in -**ou** are a bit more complicated. Normally, they have a plural ending in '-**s**':

un bisou   **des bisous**   *kisses*

but there are a small number which end in '-**x**' in their plural form. Every French child learns this list by heart:

Bijoux, cailloux, choux, genoux, hiboux, joujoux, poux.   *Jewels, pebbles, cabbages, knees, owls, toys, lice.*

OTHER PLURAL IRREGULARITIES

▶ **Mesdames et Messieurs, bonsoir !**

Some very familiar words which are made up of two words joined together behave as if they were separate words in the plural, with both parts taking the plural form. The most common ones are titles.

<u>Ma</u>dame *(Mrs)*	<u>Mes</u>dame<u>s</u>
<u>Ma</u>demoiselle *(Miss)*	<u>Mes</u>demoiselle<u>s</u>
<u>Mon</u>sieur *(Mr)*	<u>Mes</u>sieur<u>s</u>

▶ **The police are coming !**

In English we can get away with using *are* with a singular noun (e.g. *the police*) instead of *is*, because we know that more than one representative of the force will probably turn up. In French you must be strictly grammatically correct:

La police est là. *The police are here.*

But they might also say:

Les policiers arrivent. *The police officers arrive.*

Here are some other similar examples, inspired by the tendency of the French to take matters into their own hands!

<u>Le</u> peuple <u>manifeste</u> dans la rue.	*People <u>are</u> out demonstrating in the street.*
<u>Le</u> gouvernement ne <u>va</u> pas intervenir.	*The government <u>are</u> not going to intervene.*

25 Demonstrative adjectives: 'this', 'these', 'that' and 'those'

Being able to make a clear distinction between one thing and another is very important, and no more so than when shopping! Markets are perfect places to bargain and this chapter will boost your negotiating abilities.

Let's look at how to handle demonstrative adjectives and use them to get the best there is in town!

THIS, THESE: 'CE', 'CETTE', 'CET' AND 'CES'

Je voudrais ce bouteille de vin. ✗
Je voudrais <u>cette</u> bouteille de vin. ✓ *I would like this bottle of wine.*

This is how it works...

<u>un</u> poster → <u>ce</u> poster	*this poster*
<u>une</u> carte → <u>cette</u> carte	*this card*
<u>des</u> posters → <u>ces</u> posters	*these posters*
<u>des</u> cartes → <u>ces</u> cartes	*these cards*

French would not be French if there was no exception to a rule!

We need to pay particular attention to masculine (**un**) words beginning with a vowel or 'h':

un animal → ce animal ✗
un animal → <u>cet</u> animal ✓   *this animal*

In English, it is customary to change *a* to *an* before words beginning with a vowel: *an igloo, an elephant*. In French you have do something similar – the ce changes to cet. Look at the following examples:

un animal	*an animal*	**cet animal**	*this animal*
un ami	*a (male) friend*	**cet ami**	*this (male) friend*

un éléphant	an elephant	cet éléphant	this elephant
un igloo	an igloo	cet igloo	this igloo
un ouragan	a hurricane	cet ouragon	this hurricane
un orage	a storm	cet orage	this storm
un uniforme	a uniform	cet uniforme	this uniform
un hôpital	a hospital	cet hôpital	this hospital
un hôtel	a hotel	cet hôtel	this hotel
un homme	a man	cet homme	this man

The change from **ce** to **cet** makes the words flow more easily, just as the *a* to *an* change in English does. In general, two vowel sounds next to each other would be difficult to pronounce, for example: c<u>e</u> <u>é</u>léphant. The addition of the 't' separates the two vowel sounds. The letter 'h' is mostly silent (see Chapter 9). This is why we also say <u>cet</u> **homme** (*this man*) instead of c<u>e</u> **homme**.

But be careful, we say **ce harem** (*this harem*) because the 'h' in <u>h</u>arem is not silent.

THIS BOOK, THAT BOOK: 'CE LIVRE-CI', 'CE LIVRE-LÀ'

Adding -ci and -là means that you are being more specific in your reference to a particular object.

ceci	*this*	cela	*that*
ce livre-ci	<u>*this*</u> book	ce livre-là	<u>*that*</u> book
cette pomme-ci	<u>*this*</u> apple	cette pomme-là	<u>*that*</u> apple
ces bananes-ci	<u>*these*</u> bananas	ces bananes-là	<u>*those*</u> bananas
cet hôtel-ci	<u>*this*</u> hotel	cet hôtel-là	<u>*that*</u> hotel

Insight

Ci is associated with **ici** (*here*, 'the nearest to you') and là with 'là-bas' (*there*, *over there*, 'at a distance away').

Now, you are fully equipped to go shopping and have fun getting the best products!

26 Being vague: **beaucoup, quelque(s)** and **plusieurs**

Expressing *many, often, several, various, sometimes* and *a few* can cause problems.

MANY: IS IT 'BEAUCOUP DE' OR 'BEAUCOUP DES'?

Nous avons beaucoup des restaurants italiens à Manchester. ✗

Nous avons <u>beaucoup de</u> restaurants italiens à Manchester. ✓ *We have <u>many</u> Italian restaurants in Manchester.*

Nous avons <u>de nombreux</u> restaurants italiens à Manchester. ✓ *We have <u>many</u> Italian restaurants in Manchester.*

Beaucoup is <u>never</u> followed by **des**. **Beaucoup** is always followed by **de**, and is often either used on its own (e.g. **merci beaucoup**, *thank you very much*) or with abstract nouns describing time (e.g. **beaucoup de temps**, *a lot of time*), people (e.g. **beaucoup de monde**, *many people*) and non-tangible things (e.g. **beaucoup de chance**, *a lot of luck*).

> **Insight**
> Restaurants are not abstract concepts since you can physically see and count them, so using **de nombreux** or **de nombreuses** for *many* can often be more appropriate.

'QUELQUE(S)' *A FEW* AND 'PLUSIEURS' *SEVERAL*

Il a un peu de livres Sterling. ✗
Il a <u>quelques</u> livres Sterling. ✓ *He has a few pounds.*

Quelque(s) is mostly used to express *a little* or *a few*, whereas **plusieurs** always means *several*.

Elle a acheté quelques journaux en anglais pour son père. *She bought a few English newspapers for her father.*

Il a fait plusieurs erreurs d'orthographe. *He made several spelling mistakes.*

HOW TO SAY *OFTEN*, *SOMETIMES* AND *FROM TIME TO TIME*: 'SOUVENT' AND 'QUELQUEFOIS'

Nous allons en France beaucoup de fois. ✗
Nous allons <u>souvent</u> en France. ✓   *We often go to France.*
Il fait quelque temps ses courses à Auchan. ✗
Il fait <u>quelquefois</u> ses courses   *He shops in Auchan from*
  à Auchan. ✓   *time to time/occasionally.*

ABOUT, *APPROXIMATELY* AND *AROUND*

Il habite à peu près 20 kms de Paris. ✗
Il habite à <u>environ</u> 20 kms de Paris. ✓   *He lives about/around*
                                     20 km from Paris.

J'habite <u>près de</u> Paris. ✓   *I live near Paris.*
C'est <u>à peu près</u> cela. ✓   *It is almost correct.*

Près de means *close to*, and not *roughly*. This can be confused with à peu près which means *almost* or *roughly*, as shown in the above examples.

SOME, *A FEW* AND *ANY*: 'QUELQUE(S)', 'DU/DE LA/DE L'/DES', 'CERTAIN(E)(S)'

Avez-vous quelque lait ? ✗
Avez-vous du lait ? ✓   *Have you got any milk?*
Je n'ai pas du lait. ✗
Je <u>n</u>'ai <u>pas de</u> lait. ✓   *I have no milk.*
Je <u>n</u>'ai <u>aucun</u> lait. ✓   *I have not got any milk.*
Elle a acheté <u>quelques</u> livres. ✓   *She bought a few books.*
Elle a acheté <u>des</u> livres. ✓   *She bought some books.*
Oh regarde, des étudiants sont absents. ✗
Oh regarde, <u>certains</u> étudiants sont   *Oh, look, a few students*
  absents. ✓   *are absent.*

For more about how to say *some*, see Chapter 19a.

27a The present participle: the '-ing' thing (the gerund)

Coming up with the equivalent of the English -*ing* ending can be tricky in French. It has many different meanings in English. Look at the following sentence: *I am read*ing *the newspaper (while) listen*ing *to music*. Though these two -*ing* words look the same, in French we need two different ways of expressing them properly.

THE MAIN ACTIVITY: I AM READING

To translate 'I am <u>reading</u> the newspaper' it's all too tempting to look at the familiar *I am* from the verb *to be*, translate it ('je suis...'), and then find a French word for *reading*.

Je suis lecture le journal. ✗
Je suis lisant le journal. ✗

But this is too literal. *Reading* here is part of a particular English verb construction, one of two ways in which we express the here and now.

- ▶ *I read the newspaper.* (i.e. this is something I regularly do)
- ▶ *I am reading the newspaper.* (i.e. at this moment)

There is only one way of expressing both these in French, by using the present tense.

Je <u>lis</u> le journal. ✓   *I am reading/read the newspaper.*

THE PARALLEL ACTIVITY: WHILE LISTENING TO MUSIC

... **<u>en</u> écout<u>ant</u> de la musique.**

Here you are talking about doing two things at once. *While listening to music* is a secondary, parallel activity, something you do at the same time as the main activity of reading. To create this '-ing' word you replace the '-ons' of the nous form of the present tense with '-ant'.

nous écoutons	*we are listening*
en écoutant	*(while) listening*
Je lis le journal en écoutant de la musique.	*I read the paper while listening to music*
<u>En</u> travaill<u>ant</u> **maintenant, nous allons avoir du temps libre pendant le week-end.**	*By working now we'll have some free time at the weekend.*

▶ **Attention!** There are some irregulars! Here are some of the most common:

en étant	*by/while being*
en ayant	*by/while having*
en sachant	*by/while knowing*

....

Insight

This **-ant** construction can also be used as a verbal adjective (the 'gerundive') straight after a noun. It must, of course, agree with the noun:

le soleil couch<u>ant</u>	*the setting sun*
l'horloge parl<u>ante</u>	*the speaking clock*

....

IN THE PROCESS OF DOING

If you want to place a lot of emphasis on the fact that you are doing something at this very moment, you can use the expression **en train de** which, incidentally, has nothing to do with being on the train! You can say to your noisy children:

Allez jouer ailleurs ! Je suis <u>en train de</u> lire.	*Go and play somewhere else! I am (in the process of) reading.*

27b Running is hard: naming an activity

In English we name activities using '-ing': 'my hobbies are *running*, *reading* and *cooking*'. In French, you can't use the present participle (**courant, lisant, faisant la cuisine**):

Lisant et écoutant de la musique sont mes deux passe-temps préférés. ✗

Instead, to name an activity you simply use a verb in its infinitive form, which we often translate as *to read* or *to listen* (this, incidentally, would sound perfectly correct in the sentence: *I also like to read/to listen/to watch…*). No change at all is needed from the action word or verb as you find it in the dictionary, i.e. in its infinitive form.

<u>Lire</u> et <u>écouter</u> de la musique sont mes deux passe-temps préférés. ✓	*Reading and listening to music are my two favourite hobbies.*
J'aime aussi <u>regarder</u> la télévision et <u>aller</u> au cinéma. ✓	*I also like watching television and going to the cinema.*

HOLD ON, I'M COMING!

French uses the present tense to convey the immediacy of something that is about to happen, just as we do in English.

L'appétit vient en mangeant ! (Eating makes you hungry!)

**Je suis partant en France ce
  week-end. ✗**
Je pars en France ce week-end. ✓   *I am leaving for France this
                                            weekend.*

CATCH PHRASES

Look at the way these '-ing' words in English are expressed in
French:

L'appétit vient en mangeant !   *Eating gives you an appetite!
                                      (The more you have, the more
                                      you want!)*
Voir c'est croire !   *Seeing is believing!*
Ce qui est fait est fait.   *What's done is done/It's no use
                                      crying over spilt milk.*
Il brûle la chandelle par   *He is burning the candle at both
  les deux bouts.   ends.*

Insight

Time spent learning the pattern of a number of key irregular
verbs in the present tense, such as **aller** (*to go*), **venir** (*to come*),
être (*to be*), **avoir** (*to have*), **prendre** (*to take*), **mettre** (*to put*)
and **faire** (*to do/make*), just like learning your times tables as
a child, is time very well spent. These verbs will stand you in
good stead at this stage, as they enable you to say what you
are doing now, and what you will definitely be doing in the
immediate future. (See Chapter 35.)

Je <u>vais</u> partir en vacances.   *I am <u>going</u> to go on holiday.*
Il <u>va</u> retrouver sa famille   *He is <u>going</u> to meet up with
  à Paris.   his family in Paris.*

Knowing these verbs will also be indispensable later on when
you come to tackle more complex language.

28a Unlocking the secret of auxiliary verbs: **avoir**

SHOULD I USE 'AVOIR' OR 'ÊTRE' AS MY AUXILIARY VERB?

Être (*to be*) and **avoir** (*to have*) are major players in expressing actions performed and completed in the past. Choosing the right one can be a problem. In the **passé composé**, or perfect tense, there are two parts to the verb:

▶ an auxiliary verb (the present tense of either **avoir** or **être**);
▶ and a past participle (e.g. **mangé**, **bu**, **sorti**).

Look at the following examples. You will see that some of these verbs in the perfect tense use **avoir** as the auxiliary verb, and others use **être**:

Il a mangé.	*He ate/He has eaten.*
Il a bu du vin.	*He drank some wine/He has drunk some wine.*
Elle est sortie à midi.	*She went out at midday.*
Nous sommes partis de bonne heure.	*We left early.*

WHEN TO USE 'AVOIR'

If you want to say that something has happened in a sequence or as an isolated past action, **avoir** is the auxiliary verb most often used:

Hier, j'<u>ai</u> regardé la télévision.	*Yesterday I watched TV.* (from **regarder**, *to watch*)
L'année dernière, il <u>a</u> acheté une voiture.	*Last year, he bought a car.* (from **acheter**, *to buy*)
Nous <u>avons</u> fini. L'addition, s'il vous plaît !	*We have finished. The bill, please!* (from **finir**, *to finish*)
Tu n'<u>as</u> pas acheté l'ordinateur ?	*Didn't you buy the computer?* (from **acheter**, *to buy*)

So, all these verbs, and in fact the majority of all verbs, take **avoir** as their auxiliary.

THE 'PASSÉ COMPOSÉ' FOR A FINISHED ACTION

The English *did* and *have done* (i.e. two different ways of describing a finished action) are both expressed in French using the **passé composé**. What a gift!

J'ai visité le château.	*I visited/have visited the castle.*
Il a vu son voisin.	*He saw/has seen his neighbour.*

Sometimes in English we use the perfect tense although the action still continues. In French, the present tense must be used instead for actions which still continue, <u>not</u> the **passé composé**:

J'ai vécu en France depuis dix ans. ✗	
Je vis en France depuis dix ans. ✓	*I have lived in France for ten years.* (i.e. I still do live in France)
J'ai vécu dix ans en France.	*I lived in France for ten years.* (i.e. I no longer do so)

(See Chapter 29a for more about **depuis** and the present tense.)

28b Unlocking the secret of auxiliary verbs: **être**

WHEN TO USE 'ÊTRE'

Elle a allé à Paris. ✗
Elle <u>est</u> allée à Paris. ✓   *She went to Paris.*
Nous avons rentrés à minuit. ✗
Nous <u>sommes</u> rentrés à minuit. ✓   *We got home at midnight.*
Il s'a dépêché. ✗
Il s'<u>est</u> dépêché. ✓   *He hurried.*

These two main groups of verbs form their perfect tense with être:

▸ all reflexive verbs (e.g. **se lever, s'habiller**; see Chapter 16);
▸ a particular group of verbs which mainly talk about movement, or a change of state. These are listed below:

aller *to go*	**entrer** *to go in*	**partir** *to leave*	**revenir** *to come back*
arriver *to arrive*	**monter** *to go up*	**rentrer** *to go home*	**sortir** *to go out*
devenir *to become*	**mourir** *to die*	**rester** *to stay*	**tomber** *to fall*
descendre *to go down*	**naître** *to be born*	**retourner** *to return*	**venir** *to come*

There is, as you can see, a distinct difference between the kind of actions which take être and **avoir** as their auxiliary verb.

'ÊTRE' AND INTRANSITIVE VERBS

Let's consider the following examples:

Il s'est levé de sa chaise.   *He got up from his chair.*
Il est allé dans son bureau.   *He went into his office.*
Il s'est assis devant son   *He sat down in front of his*
  ordinateur.   *computer.*

If you remove the chair, the office and the computer, saying *he got up*, *he went* and *he sat down*, the remaining short sentences still have meaning. These sorts of verbs are known as 'intransitive verbs' (i.e. they do not need a direct object to make sense) and in French these intransitive verbs take **être** as the auxiliary. Therefore, if you do not need anything or anybody to make the action meaningful, use être as the auxiliary verb (e.g. **je me suis levé(e)**, *I got up;* **tu es né(e)**, *you were born;* **nous sommes arrivé(e)(s)**, *we arrived*).

Whenever être is used as the auxiliary verb, the past participle must agree with the subject of the sentence, i.e., who is doing the action.

Il est arrivé.	*He arrived /has arrived.*
Elle est arrivée.	*She arrived/has arrived.*
Il s'est lavé les mains.	*He washed his hands.*
Ils se sont lavés les mains.	*They washed their hands.*

Deciding whether a sentence makes sense without a direct object is a major clue to help you know when to use **avoir** or **être** in the past!

Insight

Some verbs listed above as taking the auxiliary verb être may take <u>either</u> être (when nobody or nothing is needed, i.e intransitively) <u>or</u> **avoir** (when something or somebody is needed, i.e. transitively). Look at these examples:

Elle est montée.	*She went up.*
Elle a monté <u>l'escalier.</u>	*She went up the stairs.*
Joseph est descendu.	*Joseph came down.*
Joseph a descendu <u>les valises</u>.	*He brought the suitcases down.*
Elle est rentrée tard.	*She came back late.*
Elle a rentré <u>la voiture</u> dans le garage.	*She put the car in the garage.*
Elle est sortie du cinéma à neuf heures.	*She left the cinema at nine o'clock.*
Elle a sorti ses lunettes de son sac.	*She took her glasses out of her bag.*

29a Talking about time: depuis, il y a ... que and ça fait ... que

SINCE WHEN HAVE YOU HAD PROBLEMS WITH 'DEPUIS'?

At its simplest the word **depuis** means *since*. If somebody asks when you started learning French, they will use **depuis** in their question. You can use the same word in your reply.

depuis le mois dernier	*since last month*
depuis mes vacances en France	*since my holiday in France*
depuis 2008	*since 2008*

You can also use **depuis** to refer to the entire period of time for which you have been learning (in English we would use the word *for*).

Pour plusieurs mois. ✗	
<u>**Depuis**</u> **quelques semaines/ plusieurs mois/un an. ✓**	*For a few weeks/several months/ a year.*

So far, so good. The problem for English speakers arises when we want to ask the question, or compose a whole sentence, rather than give a short reply. We want to say: *How long <u>have you been learning</u> French?*, *How long <u>have you learned</u> French?*, and reply *<u>I have learned/been learning</u> French for a year*.

Although this looks like a good opportunity to use the past tense (**passé composé** – formed using **avoir**, *to have*), this isn't grammatically correct in French.

Depuis combien de temps avez-vous appris le français ? ✗
J'ai appris le français depuis un an. ✗

Instead, in French when you want to ask or say how long or since when you have done something, you must use the present tense:

<u>**Depuis**</u> **combien de temps** <u>**apprenez-vous**</u> **le français ?** ✓	*How long have you been learning French?*

J'apprends le français **depuis** un an.	*I have been learning French for a year.*
Depuis combien de temps **connaissez-vous** Marie ?	*How long have you known Marie?*
Je connais Marie **depuis** son enfance.	*I have known Marie since she was a child.*
Depuis que **je lis** ce commentaire je comprends 'depuis' !	*Since reading this commentary I understand 'depuis'!*

Think of it like this. If you are still involved in an activity, then the present tense is more appropriate than a past tense, which would imply that you had stopped!

'ÇA FAIT/IL Y A … QUE'

This is an alternative way of expressing how long you have been doing something, and again you must use the present tense.

Ça fait combien de temps **que vous suivez** des cours du soir ?	*How long have you been going to evening classes?*
Ça fait longtemps **que je travaille** mon français.	*I have been working at my French for a long time.*
Il y a cinq ans que j'étudie le français.	*I have been studying French for five years.*

Insight

However, in a <u>negative statement</u> our instinct to use the perfect tense is appropriate:

Je n'ai pas parlé français depuis cinq ans.	*I haven't spoken French for five years.*
Ça fait/Il y a cinq ans que je n'ai pas parlé français.	*I haven't spoken French for five years.*

These activities are a thing of the past, and therefore it makes more sense to use the past tense.

29b Talking about time: **pour** and **pendant**

'POUR'

Pour (*for*) is a word with multiple uses. Look at the following contexts in which **pour** may be used:

Un billet s'il vous plaît.	*A ticket please.*	
<u>Pour</u> aller où ?	*Where to?*	(with an infinitive to express an intention)
<u>Pour</u> Paris.	*To Paris.*	(with a destination)
C'est <u>pour</u> vous, Madame ?	*Is it for you, Madame?*	(with a strong pronoun)
Oui, c'est <u>pour</u> moi, <u>pour</u> la santé.	*Yes, it's for me, for my health.*	(with a strong pronoun, for emphasis)

'Pour' for future planning
Sometimes you do find the word **pour** used in connection with time when future plans are being discussed.

Les enfants viennent <u>pour</u> Noël.	*The children are coming for Christmas.*
Ce sera <u>pour</u> l'année prochaine.	*That will be for next year/We'll leave that till next year.*

SHOULD I USE 'POUR' OR 'PENDANT' WHEN TALKING ABOUT THE PAST?

To introduce a length of time in the past, **pour** is never used. This is an easy mistake to make, because in English we do use the word *for*. In the following examples you will see that **pendant** can be used instead, but often an equivalent word for *for* is omitted altogether:

Nous y sommes restés pour deux nuits. ✗

Nous y sommes restés (<u>pendant</u>) deux nuits. ✓ *We stayed there for two nights.*

Nous avons voyagé en Eurostar pour deux heures et demie. ✗	
Nous avons voyagé (<u>pendant</u>) deux heures et demie en Eurostar. ✓	*We travelled by Eurostar for two and a half hours.*
Nous nous sommes promenés dans Paris pour toute une journée. ✗	
Nous nous sommes promenés dans Paris (<u>pendant</u>) toute une journée. ✓	*We walked round Paris for a whole day.*

Insight

As a general rule of thumb, use **pour** for the future and **pendant** for the past.

'PENDANT' WITH A NOUN

You certainly do need to include the word **pendant**, however, to translate *during*:

<u>Pendant</u> la nuit on entendait le bruit des jeunes dans la rue.	*<u>During</u> the night we could hear the noise of young people in the street.*
<u>Pendant</u> notre séjour tout s'est bien passé.	*Everything went well <u>during</u> our stay.*

'Pendant que' to describe a parallel activity

Use **pendant que** (*while/whilst*) to indicate a parallel activity:

Pendant que nous visitions, Paris, les enfants étaient chez les grand-parents.	*While we were visiting Paris, the children stayed with their grandparents.*

30 Il y a – there's nothing quite like it!

Il y a means *there is* or *there are*; you'll often turn automatically to this phrase, which rolls nicely off the tongue, to begin a sentence. It requires very little thought – there's no need to change it from singular to plural and it can be a really useful launching pad.

À Arcachon, <u>il y a</u> une belle plage où <u>il y a</u> plein d'activités pour les enfants.

In Arcachon <u>there is</u> a beautiful beach where <u>there are</u> lots of activities for children.

SOMETIMES 'IL Y A' NEEDS TO CHANGE

However useful, remember that il y a has to change when it is used in past, future and conditional sentences. The key to this is the understanding that the a of il y a comes from the verb avoir (*to have*), which has to change its tense:

<u>Il y avait</u> beaucoup de monde sur la plage hier.

There were a lot of people on the beach yesterday.

Demain <u>il y aura</u> moins de monde.

Tomorrow there will be fewer people.

<u>Il va y avoir</u> moins de monde car c'est la rentrée.

There are going to be fewer people because the school term starts.

Un jour <u>il y a eu</u> de l'orage.

One day there was a storm.

<u>Il y aurait</u> un restaurant sur la plage si c'était permis.

There would be a restaurant on the beach if it was allowed.

'IL N'Y A PAS'

Note the position of the negative ne...pas: the y a/y avait/y a eu/y aura/y aurait are inseparable.

Il <u>n</u>'y a <u>pas</u> de neige aujourd'hui.
Hier, il <u>n</u>'y avait <u>pas</u> de soleil.

There is no snow today.
Yesterday, it wasn't sunny.

Il n'y aura bientôt plus d'enfants du tout.

Soon there will be no children at all.

'IL Y A' *AGO*

When followed by a period of time, **il y a** also translates the English word *ago*. Used in this context, **il y a** never changes. The verbs in these sentences are always in the past tense, of course.

Nous sommes partis en vacances il y a une dizaine de jours.

We left for our holiday about ten days ago.

Il y a cinq ans nous n'avions pas assez d'argent.

Five years ago we didn't have enough money.

Insight

When you thank someone for something, they may reply:

Il n'y a pas de quoi !

Think nothing of it!

Someone may show their concern for you by asking you:

Qu'est-ce qu'il y a ?

What's the matter?/What's wrong?

31 The perfect and imperfect tenses – which to use

We need two tenses to speak in the past. Getting these two tenses mixed up is very common.

'LE PASSÉ COMPOSÉ' *THE PERFECT TENSE*

This tense is used when the action is already completed – over and done with – at the time of speaking. Look at these examples:

Je suis allé(e) à Paris.	*I went to Paris.*
Il a déjeuné.	*He ate his lunch.*
Je suis né(e) en 1948.	*I was born in 1948.*
J'ai habité en France.	*I (have) lived in France.* (i.e I did live in France, but I no longer do so)

All of these are completed actions. So far so good!

'L'IMPARFAIT' *THE IMPERFECT TENSE*

Alongside the **le passé composé** comes another tense, **l'imparfait** (the imperfect tense). This tense is used in a number of situations, to describe:

1 Recurrent actions in the past, i.e. habits in the past

J'<u>allais</u> à la plage tous les jours. *I <u>used to go</u> to the beach every day.*

2 Ongoing actions

Elle <u>parlait</u> au policier quand je suis arrivé.	*She <u>was talking</u> to the police offficer when I arrived.*

3 Background actions

Il <u>faisait</u> beau quand il est sorti.	*The weather <u>was</u> beautiful when he went out.*

4 States of mind or of the body

J'**avais** peur.	*I <u>was</u> scared.*
J'**étais** malade.	*I <u>was</u> ill.*

USING THE PERFECT AND IMPERFECT TENSES TOGETHER

Using a mixture of both past tenses together can make what you are recounting more interesting to your audience. Combining completed actions in the perfect tense (e.g. **je me suis levé**, *I got up;* **j'ai pris mon petit déjeuner**, *I had my breakfast*) with the imperfect tense allows you to set a more detailed scene:

Quand je me suis levé, le soleil brillait (*When I got up* – completed action, *the sun was shining* – background description), **mon mari dormait encore** (*my husband was still asleep* – ongoing past action), **et j'avais un mal de tête atroce** (*and I had a splitting headache* – ongoing past action).

Insight

J'**ai habité** en France pendant dix ans.	*I <u>lived</u> in France for ten years.*

I lived in France for ten years – a specified period only, and I no longer live there. In other words, because the past action was for a finite period of time and has now ceased, the perfect tense here has to be used. Now look at the difference between the English and French tenses in the following example:

Ils **sont nés** en Afrique.	*They <u>were born</u> in Africa.*

It is not possible, after all, to be born several times, so the perfect tense is always used in French. The perfect is the right tense for finished and unique actions such as **naître** (*to be born*) and **mourir** (*to die*).

32a Prepositions: choosing the correct one

Using the wrong preposition can confuse your listener! You have to make some careful and informed choices and remember not always to translate literally from English to French! Let's look at some prepositions which cause particular confusion.

'SUR' *ON* OR 'DANS' *IN*

Il est sur le train. ✗
Il est <u>dans</u> le train. ✓   *He is on the train.*

Being *on* the train in French literally means being *on the roof*! We all know how difficult it is to get a seat on the train at peak times, but in France we rarely resort to the roof! Take care to avoid this easy error.

'A' *TO, AT, IN* OR 'POUR' *FOR*

Look at the difference between these two sentences:

Je prends le train à Londres.
I catch the train in London.
(i.e. I am in London when
I take the train)

Je prends le train pour Londres.
I catch the train for London.

'SUR' *ON* OR 'À LA...'

**Carla Bruni est sur la télévision
ce soir. ✗**
**Carla Bruni passe à la télévision
ce soir. ✓**
Carla Bruni is on TV tonight.

Sur la télévision and sur la radio mean you are physically sitting on the top of the TV or the radio! However, it is possible to watch a programme about a specific subject and on a specific channel, both using sur:

**Il regarde une émission sur les
effets des changements
climatiques.**
*He watches a programme
on the effects of climate
changes.*

**Je regarde le JT (journal télévisé)
sur TF1.**
I watch the news on TF1.

'DEVANT'/'DERRIÈRE' *IN FRONT OF/BEHIND* OR 'AVANT'/'APRÈS' *BEFORE/AFTER*

Devant and derrière position you physically *in front of* or *behind* something or somebody, whereas avant and après situate an action in time.

J'habitais devant à Guildford. ✗
J'habitais avant à Guildford. ✓
*Before, I used to live in
Guildford.*

32b Prepositions: choosing the correct one

'CHEZ...' OR 'À LA...', 'À L'...', 'AU...', 'AUX'...'?

Chez is used with:

- a person's name (e.g. **chez Pierre**, *at Pierre's*; **chez vous**, *at your place*);
- a person's profession (e.g. **chez le docteur**, *at the doctor's*)
- a business, a group or a society when these still bear the name of their founder (**chez Renault, chez Dior**).

Je vais au dentiste. ✗
Je vais <u>chez</u> le dentiste. ✓   *I go to the dentist('s).*
Je vais <u>chez</u> le coiffeur.   *I go to the hairdresser('s).*
Il travaille <u>chez</u> Renault.   *He works at Renault.*

But use **à la/à l'/au/aux** for places: **Je vais au café** (*I go to the café*); **Je l'ai vu au restaurant** (*I saw him at the restaurant*); **Elle travaille à la pharmacie/à la banque** (*She works at the pharmacy/bank*).

'EN', 'À', AND 'DE' ARE DIFFICULT TO USE PROPERLY...

Il arrive en cheval. ✗
Il arrive <u>à</u> cheval. ✓   *He arrives on horseback.*
   (i.e. he rides here)

If you use **en** instead of **à** then you arrive in fancy dress, dressed up as a horse! **En** is used for all modes of transport that have an engine: **en avion** (*by plane*), **en voiture** (*by car*), **en moto** (*by motorbike*). **À** is used for everything else: **à pied** (*on foot*), **à cheval** (*on horseback*), **à vélo** (*by bicycle*).

Vous conduisez au bureau. ✗
Vous allez au bureau <u>en</u> voiture. ✓   *You drive to work.*

If you use the phrase **conduire au bureau** it will be assumed that you are driving around the office in a car – very odd!

'PAR' *BY AND* 'À TRAVERS' *THROUGH*

These prepositions are the source of many problems, as the following common errors demonstrate:

Il est par la fenêtre. ✗
Il est <u>à</u> la fenêtre. ✓   *He is (standing) by the window.*
Le TGV passe à travers Paris. ✗
Le TGV passe <u>par</u> Paris. ✓   *The TGV goes <u>through</u> Paris.*

....

Insight

Note the difference between **à travers** *(though, across, all over)* and **de travers** *(wrongly, twisted or filthy)* in the following sentences:

Les jeunes Anglais voyagent souvent <u>à travers</u> le monde.	*English younsters often travel all over the world.*
Paul est passé <u>à travers</u> champs pour rentrer chez lui.	*Paul went across the fields to go back home.*
Il a le nez <u>de travers</u>.	*He has a twisted nose.*
J'ai avalé <u>de travers</u>.	*It went down the wrong way.*
Il m'a regardé <u>de travers</u>.	*He gave me a filthy look.*
J'ai compris <u>de travers</u>.	*I misunderstood.*

....

'DE' OR 'À'?

Choosing between **de** and **à** can be tricky. Do you want **une tasse <u>de</u> thé** (*a cup of tea*) or **une tasse <u>à</u> thé** (*a teacup*)? Here are some points to guide you:

'À' is mostly used:

▶ with compound nouns, e.g. **une brosse à dents** (*a toothbrush*), **un couteau à pain** (*a bread knife*), **une pince à linge** (*a clothes peg*);
▶ to translate *on* in phrases such as **à la télé/radio** (*on the TV/radio*), **à la page 2** (*on page 2*), **à pied** (*on foot*), **à l'heure** (*on time*);
▶ to translate *by*, e.g. **laver à la main** (*to wash by hand*).

'De' can mean:

▶ *of*, e.g. **une bouteille de vin** (*a bottle of wine*);
▶ *with*, e.g. **trembler de peur** (*to tremble with fear*), **sauter de joie** (*to jump with joy*), **rougir de honte** (*to blush with shame*);
▶ *from*, e.g. **le train de Paris** (*the train from Paris*).

33 Prepositions: their presence or absence makes a difference!

In some English verbs (e.g. *to enter*) prepositions may be implied but are not needed, whereas the equivalent expressions in French do require a preposition if their meaning is not to be affected.

'DANS' *IN, INSIDE, INTO*

The meaning of the verb **monter dans** (*to get into*) changes completely if the preposition **dans** is omitted.

Nous montons la voiture.	*We carry the car up.*
Nous montons <u>dans</u> la voiture.	*We get in(to) the car.*
Je monte <u>dans</u> l'avion.	*We get in(to) the plane.*

If the verb **monter** (*to go up, to climb*) is used without the preposition **dans**, it is only possible to avoid a slight sexual connotation if you make it clear what it is you are taking up:

Je monte les valises.   *I take the suitcases upstairs.*

Let's look at another verb whose meaning changes completely if **dans** is omitted:

J'entre la chambre. ✗
J'entre <u>dans</u> la chambre. ✓   *I enter the room.*

If you miss out the word **dans** we imagine you inserting the room into something – which doesn't really make any sense!

'DESCENDRE DE' *TO COME DOWN FROM, TO GET OUT OF,* 'SORTIR DE' *TO GO OUT OF, TO LEAVE*

Here are some more examples where the meaning of verbs changes if the associated preposition is omitted:

Nous descendons le cheval.   *We take the horse down.*
Nous descendons du cheval.   *We get off the horse.*

Here, if you use **le** instead of **du** then **descendre** also means *to kill*:
We kill/slay the horse.

Il sort la gare. ✗
Il sort de la gare. ✓   *He goes out of/leaves the station.*

If you miss out the word **de**, then we imagine you carrying the
station somewhere – which, again, doesn't really make any sense!

'ATTENDRE' *TO WAIT FOR*

J'attends pour le train. ✗
J'attends le train. ✓   *I am waiting for the train.*

The notion *for* is already implied in the French verb **attendre**, so
the word *for* (**pour**) is not needed. The same is true of other verbs,
such as **demander** (*to ask for*) and **chercher** (*to look for*).

Nous cherchons pour la sortie. ✗
Nous cherchons la sortie. ✓   *We are looking for the exit.*
Il demande pour l'heure. ✗
Il demande l'heure. ✓   *He asks for the time.*

....

Insight

Whereas in English no preposition is needed, don't forget to
add **à** in French to indicate distance:

Rouen est 100 kilomètres de Paris. ✗
Rouen est <u>à</u> 100 kilomètres de Paris. ✓

À is also used in expressions of speed:

La voiture roule <u>à</u> 120 kilomètres   *The car travels at*
   à l'heure.   *120 kilometres per hour.*

....

34a Prepositions and places: towns and regions

In this jet-setting age, it is important to be able to talk about your travel plans and experiences with confidence. A few simple guidelines will enable you to do just this. Let's start with your immediate locality.

TOWNS

'À' *to, in*

Whether you wish to say that you are going to, or staying or living in a named city, town or village, the preposition à is almost invariably the one to use.

Je vais en Londres. ✗	
Je vais <u>à</u> Londres. ✓	*I am going <u>to</u> London.*
J'habite en Manchester. ✗	
J'habite <u>à</u> Manchester. ✓	*I live <u>in</u> Manchester.*

'En'

If you are being less specific, <u>en</u> ville is used.

Je vais rester quelques heures <u>en</u> ville.	*I am going to stay <u>in</u> town for a few hours.*

'Dans'

Sometimes you will hear people say: **J'habite <u>dans</u> Paris, dans la ville même.** This means that they live in the heart of the place they have mentioned.

ENGLISH COUNTIES AND REGIONS

'Dans le' *in*

When counties and regions keep their English names they are, conveniently, always masculine, so use **dans le**:

Guildford se trouve en Surrey. ✗	
Guildford se trouve <u>dans le</u> Surrey. ✓	*Guildford is in Surrey.*
Guildford se trouve <u>dans le</u> Surrey, <u>dans le</u> sud-est de l'Angleterre. ✓	*Guildford is in Surrey, in the South East of England.*

'En'

When any region has acquired its own French name, then it may be feminine or masculine. The French names of these regions just have to be learned along with their genders. Most US states take a masculine gender in French, but there are exceptions, e.g. **la Californie, la Virginie, la Floride, la Géorgie.**

Quand je prends mes vacances en   *On holiday in England I go to*
Angleterre, je vais <u>en</u> Cornouaille (f.).   *Cornwall.*

FRENCH REGIONS AND 'DÉPARTEMENTS'

French regions and **départements** (the equivalent of counties) may either be masculine or feminine. As with the names of English counties and regions, use **dans le** with masculine names, and **en** with feminine names:

Je vais <u>en</u> Normandie (f.) **et ensuite**   *I am going to Normandy and*
  <u>dans le</u> Lot (m.).   *then to the Lot.*
Nous avons passé une semaine en   *We spent a week in Brittany*
  Bretagne (f.) **et ensuite quelques**   *and then a few days in the*
  jours dans le Cantal (m.)**, en**   *Cantal, in the Auvergne.*
  Auvergne (f.).

MOUNTAIN REGIONS

France boasts four main mountainous areas, popular with walkers and ski enthusiasts. When refering specifically to these, **dans** is the preposition to use whether you are on your way or already there enjoying the snow.

L'hiver, je vais toujours aux Alpes. ✕
L'hiver, je vais toujours dans les   *In winter, I always go to the Alps.*
  Alpes. ✓
L'été, on se promène dans le   *In summer, we go walking in the*
  Jura/le Massif Central.   *Jura/Massif Central.*

If you want to make a more general reference to the sort of area you are visiting, use **à la mer** (*to the sea*), **à la campagne** (*to the country(side)*) or **à la montagne** (*to the mountains*).

34b Prepositions and places: countries and continents

INTERNATIONAL TRAVEL

How to say *to* and *in*

Now the fun begins! Let's start by remembering that every country is either masculine or feminine, and singular or plural. Look at the table below and note the prepositions you need to say *to* or *in*:

f. singular	f. plural	m. singular	m. plural
la France *France*	**les Antilles** *the West Indies*	**le Luxembourg** *Luxembourg*	**les États-Unis** *the USA*
en France *in/to France*	**aux Antilles** *in/to the West Indies*	**au Luxembourg** *in/to Luxembourg*	**aux États-Unis** *in/to the USA*

Look at the language in action:

L'été, je pars toujours en Espagne (f.sing.).	*In summer I always go to Spain.*
Je suis allé une fois au Canada (m.sing.).	*I once went to Canada.*
Je suis resté trois mois aux États-Unis (m.pl.).	*I stayed in the States for three months.*

But notice the exception to this rule, where the name of a country begins with a vowel:

Je ne suis jamais allé au Iran (m.). ✗
Je ne suis jamais alle en Iran. ✓   *I have never been to Iran.*

> **Insight**
>
> When in doubt, assume that a country is feminine and use *en*; you will be right in the majority of cases.

How to say *from*

Wherever you come from, **de** is the preposition to use with towns and feminine countries, but **du** with masculine countries, such as **le Canada**.

Mon mari vient de Canada. ✗	
Mon mari vient du Canada. ✓	*My husband comes from Canada.*
Je viens de Londres, donc je viens d'Angleterre.	*I come from London, hence I come from England.*

To and *from*

Après de superbes vacances j'ai voyagé de France (f.) **en Angleterre** (f.).	*After a fantastic holiday I travelled back from France to England.*
Ensuite j'ai voyagé du Mexique (m.) **au Canada** (m.).	*Then I travelled from Mexico to Canada.*

INTER-CONTINENTAL TRAVEL: HOW TO SAY *IN* AND *TO*

Travelling from continent to continent is delightfully simple, like a round-the-world ticket, since the preposition **en** is always used, and there are no definite articles (**le/la/l'/les**) to consider.

J'ai voyagé en Europe, en Amérique du sud et du nord, en Afrique et en Asie – et aussi en Australie !	*I have travelled in/to Europe, South and North America, Africa and Asia – and Australia as well!*

35 Verbs worth a closer look: **attendre**, **chercher**, **venir**, **arriver**, **aller** and **partir**

Many French verbs sound or look similar to equivalent words in English. However, be careful: they may not have exactly the same meaning! Let's look at some examples:

'ATTENDRE' *TO WAIT (FOR)*

Attendre only means *to wait for* something or somebody:

J'attends le bus.	*I am waiting for the bus.*
Ils attendent leurs amis.	*They are waiting for their friends.*

However, to attend something (e.g. a meeting), use **assister à**:

J'attends un cours de français. ✗	
J'assiste à une conférence. ✓	*I attend a conference.*

If you say **J'attends un cours de français**, you imply that you are waiting for the course to become available (e.g. before you can enrol). This may not be what you intended.

'CHERCHER' *TO LOOK FOR, TO PICK UP*

The word *for* is already included in the verb **chercher**:

Nous <u>cherchons</u> un bon film.	*We are <u>looking for</u> a good film.*

Insight

We are often too quick to use **pour** to translate the English *for* – but it may not make sense if you do. **Pour** in French can indeed mean *for*, but it also often means *in order to*:

Les Anglais vivent <u>pour</u> travailler alors que les Français travaillent <u>pour</u> vivre.	*The English live in order to work whereas the French work in order to live.*

There is a tendency is to translate *to collect/pick up* with **prendre** (*to take*) or **ramasser** (literally *to pick up*, i.e. off the ground). If you use **prendre** instead of **chercher**, there is a slight sexual ambiguity, so be careful. Look at these examples:

Ramasse Roger à la gare. ✗
Va prendre Roger à la gare. ✗
Va chercher Roger à la gare. ✓   *Pick up Roger at the station.*

'VENIR' *TO COME* OR 'ARRIVER' *TO ARRIVE*?

Je viens. ✗
J'arrive. ✓   *I'm coming.*
Je viens avec vous.   *I'm coming with you.*
Je viens acheter un stylo.   *I've come (i.e. in order to) to buy a pen./I'm here to buy a pen.*
Je viens de Glasgow.   *I come <u>from</u> Glasgow.*

'Venir de'

Venir de is also used to say that you *have just done* something:

Je suis juste rentré de France.   *I have only come back from France.* (i.e. not from anywhere else)
Je <u>viens de</u> rentrer de France.   *I have <u>just</u> come back from France.*
J'ai juste acheté un stylo.   *I have only bought a pen.* (i.e. nothing else)
Je <u>viens d</u>'acheter un stylo.   *I have <u>just</u> bought a pen.*

'ALLER' *TO GO* OR 'PARTIR' *TO LEAVE*?

Je vais. ✗
Je pars ! / J'y vais ! ✓   *I am going/I'm off!*

Je vais is incomplete if you do not specify where you are going or what you are going to do:

Je vais à Lille.   *I am going to Lille.*
Nous allons en Écosse.   *We're going to Scotland.*
Il va manger.   *He is going to eat.*

(For more about **aller** and expressing future intention, see Chapter 27b.)

36 How about 'that': use **que** to express what you imagine, think, believe and feel

'IMAGINER QUE' *TO IMAGINE (THAT)*, 'PENSER QUE' *TO THINK (THAT)*, 'CROIRE QUE' *TO BELIEVE (THAT)* AND 'CONSIDÉRER QUE' *TO THINK (THAT)*

As English speakers we are often lazy about including the word *that* after verbs like *to think*, *to believe*, *to imagine* and *to feel*, to the extent that it now sounds rather formal to include it. In French, however, we have no choice but to use the word **que** (*that*) to complete such sentences since to omit it would leave the two parts of the sentence disconnected from each other. The word **que** (or **qu'** before a vowel or mute 'h') forms the necessary link.

J'imagine je rêve presque toujours (pendant) la nuit. ✗	
J'imagine que je rêve presque toujours (pendant) la nuit. ✓	*I imagine (that) I almost always dream during the night.*
Je pense j'ai rêvé cette nuit. ✗	
Je pense que j'ai rêvé cette nuit. ✓	*I think (that) I dreamed last night.*
Je crois j'ai déjà presque oublié ce rêve. ✗	
Je crois que j'ai déjà presque oublié ce rêve. ✓	*I think (that) I have already nearly forgotten that dream.*

Don't forget the **que** even when you put an adverb after the verb:

Je considère toujours qu'il exagère.	*I always think he's exaggerating.*

'SAVOIR QUE' *TO KNOW (THAT),* **'ESPÉRER QUE'** *TO HOPE (THAT),* **'SE RAPPELLER QUE'** *TO REMEMBER (THAT)* **AND 'OUBLIER QUE'** *TO FORGET THAT*

With these verbs **que** is again needed:

Mon ami <u>espère que</u> son rêve récurrent n'est pas prémonitoire.

My friend hopes (that) his recurrent dream is not a premonition.

Dans son rêve il <u>sait</u> qu'il a tué quelqu'un, mais il ne sait pas qui !

In his dream he knows (that) he has killed someone but he doesn't know who!

Il <u>se rappelle</u> qu'il a caché l'arme du crime dans une armoire.

He remembers (that) he hid the murder weapon in a wardrobe.

Il <u>a oublié</u> qu'il m'a déjà raconté ce rêve.

He has forgetten that he has already told me about this dream.

'SEMBLER QUE' *TO SEEM THAT,* **'PARAÎTRE QUE'** *TO APPEAR THAT*

In the French expressions **il semble que** (*it seems that*) and **il paraît que** (*it appears that*), the word **que** is compulsory too:

<u>Il paraît qu</u>'il oublie beaucoup de choses.

Apparently he forgets a lot of things.

Insight

Here are some responses to express an opinion:

J'imagine que oui/non !	*I imagine so/not!*
Je pense/je sais que oui !	*I think so/I know so!*
Je crois que oui !	*I think so!* (i.e. I believe so)
Je crois que non !	*I think not!* (i.e. I believe not)
Lui, il croit/espère que non !	*He thinks/hopes not!*

Choosing the right words

37 Visiting places and people: who to bring and what to take?

'VISITER' *TO VISIT*, 'RENDRE VISITE À' *TO VISIT* OR 'ALLER VOIR' *TO GO AND SEE*

You are planning a visit to places and people. Life would be simple if you could use the verb **visiter** in every situation, but this verb really means *having a good look round* and can therefore reasonably only be used for places. Use **rendre visite à**, or **aller voir**, for people.

Je vais visiter mes amis. ✗	
Je vais <u>aller voir</u> mes amis. ✓	*I am going to see my friends.*
Je vais <u>rendre visite à</u> mes amis. ✓	*I am going to visit my friends.*
Je vais <u>visiter</u> des musées à Paris. ✓	*I am going to visit some galleries/museums in Paris.*

'LE DÉPART' *THE DEPARTURE*

When you're about to set off, beware another false friend. You can use **le départ** to discuss details (e.g. time, destination) of a flight or train, but you cannot turn it into a verb:

Nous allons départir bientôt. ✗	
Nous allons bientôt partir. ✓	*We are going to leave soon.*
C'est l'heure du départ. ✓	*It's time to leave.*

BRINGING TO AND *TAKING* FROM

Paying visits to other people can be complicated – should you take a gift, and if so what and could you take along a friend too? Amongst this uncertainty it may help to remember that the prefix **a-** implies 'towards', and the prefix **em-** implies 'away from'. So:

▶ use **amener** to <u>bring</u> (*somebody*), and **apporter** to <u>bring</u> (*something*) <u>to</u> a place;

► use **emmener** to _take (somebody)_, and **emporter** to _take (something)_ _from_ a place.

On apporte le bébé ? ✗	
On <u>amène</u> le bébé ? ✓	_Shall we bring the baby?_
<u>Emmène</u> ta copine !	_Take your friend away (with you)!_
<u>Amène</u> ta copine !	_Bring your friend along with you!_
On <u>apporte</u> des fleurs	_Shall we take flowers or chocolates?_
ou des chocolats ?	

You turn up with flowers, the baby and your girlfriend. Your host says:

C'est bien ! Tu as amené ta	_That's good! You've brought your_
copine !	_girlfriend!_

The following sentences will reinforce the correct usage of these verbs:

Si tu <u>amènes</u> le bébé, <u>apporte</u> aussi sa poussette parce qu'on va vous <u>emmener</u> voir les parents. Nous passons acheter une pizza à <u>emporter</u>. _If you bring the baby, bring the buggy with you too because we are going to take you (out) to see my parents. We're calling in to buy a take-away pizza on the way._

Insight

Amener is often wrongly used by native speakers! You might hear people say, for example, **J'amène une bouteille**, when **J'apporte une bouteille** (_I'll bring a bottle_) would be correct.

38 Choose your verbs carefully!

'CONNAÎTRE' OR 'SAVOIR'?

Both these verbs mean *to know* in English, but they are not
interchangeable. Look at these examples:

Je <u>connais</u> bien Paris.	*I know Paris well.*
Oui, je <u>connais</u> Jean.	*Yes, I know Jean.*
Je <u>sais</u> qui vous êtes.	*I know who you are.*
Il <u>sait</u> parler espagnol.	*He knows how to speak Spanish.*
La télé est en panne. Le <u>sais</u>-tu ?	*Do you know the TV is broken?*
Oui, je le <u>sais</u>.	*Yes, I know.*

So, **savoir** means:

▶ to know how to do something: **Il sait (comment) nager.**
  (*He knows how to swim.*)
▶ to know a fact, or reason: **savoir quelque chose** (*to know
  something*), **savoir pourquoi/où/quand...** (*to know why/
  where/when...*)

Connaître means:

▶ to know people, places, works of art and literature, etc.

'POUVOIR' OR 'SAVOIR'?

Pouvoir (*to be able to*) and **savoir** (*to know how to*) are easy to
confuse since they both mean much the same thing.

Il sait apprendre. ✓	*He can* (i.e. he knows how to) *learn.*
Il peut apprendre. ✓	*He is able to learn.*

But look at the difference between the following:

Pouvez-vous parler	*Can you speak?* (e.g. after injuring your mouth).
Savez-vous parler Français ?	*Can you speak French?*

'ENTENDRE' *TO HEAR* OR 'ÉCOUTER' *TO LISTEN*?

J'entends le bruit de la radio.	*I hear the noise of the radio.*
J'écoute les nouvelles à la radio.	*I listen to the news on the radio.*

'VOIR' *TO SEE* OR 'REGARDER' *TO LOOK AT*?

Je vois mon père, là-bas.	*I see my father, over there.*
Je regarde souvent la télévision française.	*I often watch French TV.*

'LAISSER', 'PARTIR' OR 'QUITTER'? ARE YOU JUST GOING, OR LEAVING FOR GOOD?

They all mean *to leave* in English, but **partir** is used to for leaving a place to go somewhere else, and **laisser** means *to leave (behind) (something/somebody)*. **Quitter** means you've left someone for good.

Il part de/quitte Paris à six heures.	*He leaves Paris at six o'clock.*
Il a laissé son pull chez moi.	*He has left his jumper at my house.*
Elle a quitté son mari.	*She has left her husband.* (i.e. for good)

....

Insight

▶ If your ears or eyes are functioning properly, you *hear well* and *see well* (**entendre bien** and **voir bien**):

Malgré ses quatre-vingts-dix ans, il entend bien.	*Despite being ninety, he hears well.*

▶ but when you are *listening well* (i.e. carefully) and *paying attention*, use **écouter attentivement** (*to listen carefully*) and **regarder attentivement** (*to watch carefully*):

La fille écoute attentivement son professeur.	*The girl listens carefully to her teacher.*

....

39a Qualifications and achievements: passing and taking exams

Talking about schooling and training requires special skills! Here are some areas of language that need particular attention.

'LES DIPLÔMES' *QUALIFICATIONS*

'Obtenir' *to get, to gain* **or 'gagner'** *to win, to earn*?
There is no logic here: why do we *win* an award in English, but *obtain* an award or qualification in French!

J'ai gagné une bourse. ✗
J'ai obtenu une bourse. ✓   *I won/gained/got a scholarship.*

In French, **gagner une bourse** would mean that the scholarship was obtained as a consequence of a lucky strike in a gambling operation! Strangely, and against any logic, **on gagne sa vie** (*one earns a living*). **Gagner** is mainly used in the following situations:

▶ where there is an element of chance, e.g. **je gagne au loto** (*I win the lottery*);
▶ where something is being saved, e.g. **je gagne du temps** (*I save time*);
▶ where there is an element of chance and reward, e.g. **je gagne bien ma vie** (*I earn a good living*).

Do you study for 'une licence' or 'un degré'?
J'étudie pour un degré. ✗
Je fais une licence. ✓   *I study for a degree.*

Un degré is a measure of temperature, or a level; it is never used to refer to a degree qualification.

How do you take an exam: 'prendre' or 'passer'?
J'ai pris un examen. ✗
J'ai passé un examen. ✓   *I took/sat an exam.*

An exam cannot be caught as one catches a bus (**prendre le bus**)!
Passer does not indicate whether you have passed or failed, just
that you sit an exam. There are two possible outcomes of sitting an
exam: **réussir** (*to pass*) or **échouer** and **rater** (*to fail*).

Il a réussi son examen/Il a été reçu à son examen.	*He passed his exam.*
C'est dommage, elle a échoué/ raté l'examen.	*It's a shame, she has failed the exam.*

Insight

Les écoliers (*school children*, aged 6–11) attend l'école
(primaire) (*primary school*).

> Les écoliers vont à l'école.

Les collégiens (*school children*, aged 11–15) attend le collège
(*secondary school*).

> Les collégiens vont au collège.

Les lycéens (*school children*, aged 15–18) attend le lycée
(*secondary school*).

> Les lycéens vont au lycée.

Everyone who studies under a teacher can be called **un/une
élève** (*pupil/student*) whether they are a child or an adult.
If you do not belong to one of the above institutions, you
may consider yourself **un étudiant** (*student*).

You may have heard of **les écoles préparatoires.** They are
special colleges where students prepare for the very selective
entrance exams for **les grandes écoles** – prestigious universities,
which are roughly the French equivalent of the top university
and research institutions found in other countries, such as
Oxford, Cambridge and Harvard.

39b Au travail *the workplace*

'UNE POSITION' OR 'UN POSTE'?

Je veux cette position. ✗
Je veux ce poste. ✓   *I want this position.*

Une position in French always refers to the shape your body
can take (**position assise**, *seated*; **position debout**, *standing*).
You cannot apply for one!

HOW TO APPLY FOR A JOB: 'POSER' OR 'APPLIQUER'?

To apply for a position, use the phrase **poser sa candidature**, not
appliquer which refers to the application of an ointment.

INTERVIEWS

'Les interviews', 'les entretiens'
Les interviews and **les entretiens** are for the rich and famous! If you
are a journalist, you are <u>granted</u> one, but if you are famous you
<u>give</u> one:

Marconna m'a accordé une   *Marconna has agreed to give me*
  interview/un entretien.   *an interview.*
Carla Bruni donne une interview/ *Carla Bruni gives an interview to*
  un entretien à la presse.   *the press.*

There is very little difference between **une interview** and **un
entretien**, although **un entretien** may refer more to interviews
where discussions and talks take place.

How are you called for your interview?
Je suis invité à une interview
  demain. ✗
Je suis convoqué à <u>un entretien</u> *I have been invited to a job*
  d'embauche demain. ✓   *interview tomorrow.*

J'ai un entretien d'embauche demain. ✓   *I have a job interview tomorrow.*

You are never 'invited' to a job interview in French. **Inviter** (*to invite*) is usually associated with pleasurable and stress-free occasions, such as in the phrase **inviter quelqu'un à dîner** (*to ask someone to dinner*), or, for example, if you are offering to pay for a meal in a restaurant, you might say: **Je t'invite/Je vous invite** (*It is my treat*). Instead, **convoquer** (*to ask to attend*) is the term used in formal, more official situations such as job interviews, or interviews with the police.

Il est <u>convoqué</u> au commissariat de police à dix heures.   *He has been called for/asked to attend a police interview at ten o'clock.*

MEETINGS

As for **les entrevues**, **les rendez-vous** and **les réunions** (all *meetings*), they occur in the work place, once you have started working. **Une entrevue** or **un rendez-vous (d'affaires)** are the words usually used to describe a business or work-related meeting between two people.

J'ai demandé une entrevue à mon patron.   *I asked to see my boss.*

Il est occupé. Il a un rendez-vous à 14h00.   *He is busy. He has a (private) meeting at 2.00 p.m.*

The word **réunion** only refers to a business, a work-related or a social meeting attended by a team/group of employees, people or friends sharing a common interest.

Monsieur Dupond ne peut pas vous parler, il est en réunion.   *Mr Dupond cannot talk to you. He is in a meeting.*

39c Les affaires *business matters*

'MON CHEF', 'MON PATRON', 'MON DIRECTEUR'... WHO DO I WORK FOR? IT DOES MY HEAD IN!

Ma nouvelle tête n'est pas sympa. ✗
Mon nouveau chef n'est pas sympa. ✓ *My new head/boss is not nice.*
La tête d'État du pays n'est pas populaire. ✗
Le chef d'État du pays n'est pas populaire. ✓   *The head of State of the country is not popular.*

The word **chef** is not restricted to a restaurant; the boss of any company, state or team is **un chef**, including **le chef cuisinier** (*the head of the kitchen*). **Chef** is therefore used when you are talking from within a company.

La tête is either used to talk about the physical part of the body (e.g. **J'ai mal à la tête**, *I have a headache*) or about an object (e.g. **la tête du lit**, the headboard). However, it is possible to say **Je suis à la tête d'une petite entreprise** (*I am the head of a small company*).

> **Insight**
>
> The title of the top-ranking person at work depends on the size of the company:
>
> ▶ if you work in a small company (**une petite entreprise**), he/she will be **le/la patron(ne)**;
> ▶ if you are employed in a larger company (**une PME: une petite et moyenne entreprise**) or a multinational company (**une grande entreprise** or **une multinationale**), then the top person will be **le Pdg** (**le président directeur général**, *the chief executive*).
> ▶ In French companies, there usually exist strict staff hierarchies amongst **les membres du personnel** (*members of staff*). Typically, first comes **le directeur** (*head*), followed by **les chefs de service** (*department managers*), **les gestionnaires de projet** or **les responsables de projet** (*project managers*), closely followed by **les attachés** (*assistants*).

ROLES, PROFESSIONS AND JOBS

When you are describing a person's role or profession, remember to leave out the words **un/une**:

Voilà Maigret. Il est inspecteur de police.	*Here's Maigret. He is a detective.*
Je suis étudiante et mère de famille.	*I am a student and a mother.*

BEWARE WORK-RELATED FALSE FRIENDS!

A word of caution! **Une affaire** rarely means *an affair*! Look at the following examples:

C'est une bonne/mauvaise affaire !	*It's a good/bad deal!*
le monde des affaires	*the business world*
un homme/une femme d'affaires	*a businessman/woman*

Un avertissement does not mean 'advertisment'! In French, **un avertissement** is *a warning* – not quite the same thing! The word for *advertising* is **la publicité**:

Il n'y a plus de publicité à la télé après 20h00.	*There is no more advertising on the TV after eight p.m.*

Unless you come from Belgium, **un mobile** is rarely used for *a mobile phone*, although the phrase **la téléphonie mobile** means *the mobile telephone industry*. The usual word for *mobile phone* is **un portable**:

Passe-moi ton portable, s'il te plaît !	*Give me your mobile, please!*

In Belgium, **un mobile** or **un GSM** are used for *mobile phone*. Your **numéro de perso** is your *mobile phone number*.

La technologie digitale est fantastique ! ✗	
La technologie numérique est fantastique ! ✓	*Digital technology is great!*

Digital only refers to our toes and fingers, e.g. **une empreinte digitale** (*fingerprint*).

40 Prendre, mettre and faire: how to deal with *taking, putting (on), doing* and *making*!

Prendre, mettre and faire are very versatile verbs and can be used in many different contexts. It is worthwhile, therefore, seeing what they can do for you!

J'ai le petit déjeuner. ✗
Je prends mon petit déjeuner. ✓   *I am having breakfast.*

Prendre can also mean:

▶ *to have*, e.g. **Je prends une douche** (*I am having a shower*);
▶ *to make*, in 'to make an appointment', e.g. **Je prends (un) rendez-vous** (*I make an appointment*);
▶ *to take*, e.g. **Nous prenons l'avion** (*We are catching a plane/ flying*).

'PRENDRE' OR 'METTRE'?

Do you take time, or put time aside, to do something? Mettre and prendre can both mean *to take*. Here are a few examples of common errors:

Je prends dix minutes pour aller
   au bureau. ✗
Je <u>mets</u> dix minutes pour aller   *It takes me ten minutes to go to*
   au bureau. ✓   *the office.*

So, in French you put aside some of your time to do something. Prendre is used for getting hold of something:

Il <u>prend</u> son manteau.   *He takes his coat (with him).*
Je <u>prends</u> le journal sur la table.   *I pick up the newspaper from*
                                          the table.

Mettre can also mean *to put* or *to put on*:

Je <u>mets</u> mon téléphone dans ma poche.   *I put my telephone in my pocket.*
Il <u>met</u> son pull.   *He puts (on) his jumper.*

'FAIRE' OR 'JOUER'?

When talking about sports, **jouer à** (*to play*) and **faire de** (here, *to play* or *to practise*) are subtly different:

Je joue au tennis chaque jour.   *I play tennis every day.*
Je fais du tennis.   *I play tennis. (i.e. it is one of the sports I play)*

So, the phrase **faire du tennis** means that you play tennis as a sport, but use **jouer au tennis** to mean more specifically that you play twice a week, or on Saturdays. In other words **faire de**, rather than **jouer à**, is often used in French when talking about the sporting activities one does in general. Look at the difference in meaning between these sentences:

Je <u>fais</u> du foot.   *I play football. (i.e. it's one of my hobbies)*

Il <u>joue</u> au rugby le lundi.   *He plays rugby on Mondays.*
Paul est absent, il <u>fait</u> du tennis. ✗
Paul est absent, il <u>joue</u> au tennis. ✓   *Paul is not here right now, he is playing tennis.*

The second sentence is more correct as it indicates that Paul is actually in the process of playing a game of tennis at the present moment.

Insight

Note the uses of **jouer de** (*to play*, with musical instruments), **faire de** and **jouer dans** in the following examples:

Elle joue du piano, du violon, de la guitare et de la harpe.   *She plays the piano, violin, guitar and harp.*
Pierre est acteur. Il fait du théâtre depuis vingt ans et il a joué dans de nombreuses pièces importantes.   *Pierre is an actor. He has been acting for twenty years and has acted in many important plays.*

41 Être or avoir, *being* or *having*? How old are you and how do you feel?

'QUEL ÂGE AVEZ VOUS ?' *HOW OLD ARE YOU?*

In English we 'are' the age that we are, but in French we clock up a certain number of years, like notches on a belt, and **avoir** (*to have*) is the verb to use – maybe making it less difficult to shed unwanted years!

Quel âge es-tu ? ✗	
Quel âge <u>as</u>-tu ? ✓	*How old are you?*
Je suis dix-huit. ✗	
J'<u>ai</u> dix-huit ans. ✓	*I am eighteen.*

Most people acquire this particular soundbite early on in their learning, but it's all too easy to revert to using **être** when talking about age in the future or past, instead of the correct other tenses of **avoir**.

Romeo était vingt ans. ✗	
Romeo <u>avait</u> vingt ans. ✓	*Romeo was twenty.*
Juliette va bientôt être dix-neuf. ✗	
Elle <u>va</u> bientôt <u>avoir</u> dix-neuf ans. ✓	*Juliette is going to be nineteen soon.*

EXPRESSING ELEMENTAL FEELINGS

Like age, some elemental, instinctive feelings such as being hungry, thirsty, cold and hot are conveyed in French using the verb **avoir**, <u>not</u> être. If you use être with **chaud** or **froid**, the sense is rather different.

For our young lovers, things are not going well!

De retour dans son appartement il est chaud mais elle est froide.	*Back at his flat he is keen but her manner is chilly.*

Grammatically this is not incorrect and you could use être in this sentence, but the problem then couldn't be solved by just putting on an extra jumper! Look at the difference:

De retour chez lui il <u>a chaud</u> mais elle <u>a froid</u>. ✓   *When they get back to his house he feels <u>hot</u> but she feels <u>cold</u>.*

Elle a froid, ou elle est froide ? (Is she cold, or is she frigid ?)

Avoir … faim (*to be hungry*), **soif** (*to be thirsty*), **froid** (*to be cold*), **chaud** (*to be hot*), **envie** (*to desire/to want*), **raison** (*to be right*), **tort** (*to be wrong*), **besoin** (*to need*), **peur** (*to be frightened*) and **honte** (*to be ashamed*): all of these are singular nouns, so there is no change to their ending. Hopefully, for our young couple, things might work out in the end!

Ils avaient faims et soifs, donc ils sont sortis au restaurant. ✗

Ils <u>avaient faim</u> et <u>soif</u>, donc ils sont sortis au restaurant. ✓   *They were hungry and thirsty, so they went out for a meal.*

Ils <u>ont envie</u>, tous les deux, de vivre ensemble.   *They both want to move in together.*

Le père de Romeo dit qu'il <u>a tort</u>.   *Romeo's father says he is wrong.*

En fait, ils <u>ont besoin</u> d'argent ! Quelle histoire !   *Actually, they need (some) money!*

42 Faire or faire faire?

'FAIRE'

Faire is a widely used verb, *to do/make* e.g. **faire de la natation** (*to swim*), **faire la queue** (*to queue*), **faire la vaisselle** (*to do the washing up*), **faire un discours** (*to make a speech*).

Je <u>fais</u> une promenade/un tour à pied.	*I am going for a walk.*

Faire une promenade or faire un tour can be done à pied (*on foot*), à cheval (*on a horse*), à vélo (*on a bicycle*), à/en moto (*on a bike*), en bateau (*in a boat*), en bus (*in a bus*).

Faire can also mean *to pay* in the context of 'to pay attention to' or 'to be careful'.

Soigne ta petite sœur. ✗	
Regarde ta petite sœur. ✗	
Fais attention à ta petite sœur.	*Take good care of your baby*
Prends soin de ta petite sœur. ✓	*sister.*

Soigner means *to look after* someone or something (e.g. a plant) when that person or thing is unwell. As for **regarder**, it does not mean *to watch* as in 'to watch over'. Note that *Be careful!* is **Faites attention !** or **Fais attention !**

You cannot, however, 'make' a holiday in French; instead you 'spend' a holiday:

Je fais mes vacances en Écosse. ✗	
Je <u>passe</u> mes vacances dans le sud de la France. ✓	*I spend my holidays in the south of France.*

DO YOU DO IT YOURSELF OR DO YOU HAVE IT DONE? THE 'FAIRE' OR 'FAIRE FAIRE' AFFAIR!

Il répare sa voiture au garage. ✗	
Il fait réparer sa voiture au garage. ✓	*He has his car repaired at the garage.*

So, **faire faire** means *to have something done*, i.e. by somebody else. Don't make the common mistake of saying, for example, that you go to the garage and work on your car yourself, or that you go to the hairdresser and cut your hair yourself!

Je coupe mes cheveux chez le coiffeur. ✗	
Je me fais couper les cheveux chez le coiffeur. ✓	*I have my hair cut at the hairdresser's.*
Je fais construire une maison.	*I am having a house built.*
Je construis ma maison.	*I'm building my house (myself).*
Il fait peindre sa maison.	*He has his house painted.*
Il peint sa maison.	*He paints his house (himself).*

··

Insight

Faire is also used in phrases about making errors and mistakes:

Il a fait trois fautes d'orthographe.	*He made three spelling mistakes.*
Il fait erreur.	*He is making a mistake.*

Here are a few set expressions worth remembering:

Je n'en ai rien à faire.	*I do not care.*
Ne vous en faites pas !	*Do not worry!*
On s'y fait.	*One gets used to it.*
Fais voir/Faites voir !	*Show me!*

··

43 Le temps *weather* and *time* – taking the time to sort them out!

'LE TEMPS' *WEATHER*

'Le temps' and 'faire'

Le temps is the only French word for *weather*, and **faire** is the verb most frequently used to describe it. If you say **C'est froid !**, you could be talking about many things, but not the weather!

Quel temps est-il ? ✗	
Quel temps fait-il ? ✓	*What is the weather like?*
Il est un temps magnifique en Provence. ✗	
Il <u>fait</u> un temps magnifique en Provence. ✓	*The weather is wonderful in Provence.*
Normalement il <u>fait</u> beau, il <u>fait</u> du soleil et il <u>fait</u> chaud.	*It is usually fine, sunny and hot.*
Quelquefois il <u>fait</u> du vent, il <u>fait</u> froid, et il <u>fait</u> mauvais.	*Sometimes it is windy, cold and unpleasant.*

'Le temps' and 'être'

Only when a sentence about the weather begins with the words le temps is it followed by the verb **être**, or another verb altogether, but not **faire**.

Le temps fait beau. ✗	
Le temps <u>est</u> bon. ✓	*The weather is nice.*
Le temps <u>va</u> changer.	*The weather is going to change.*

> **Insight**
> Remember: use either le temps est..., or il fait...

'il y a...' *there is..., there are...*

A lot of weather expressions start with **il y a...**

Il y a des nuages, il y a du vent,   *It's cloudy, it's windy, it's sunny,*
   il y a du soleil, il y a de la neige,   *it's snowy, it's foggy.*
   il y a du brouillard.

'Pleuvoir' *to rain*, **'grêler'** *to hail* and **'neiger'** *to snow*
With these verbs, both **faire** and **être** are redundant (together with
your suncream!).

Il fait pluie, il fait grêle et il fait
   neige. ✗
Il pleut, il grêle et il neige. ✓   *It's raining, it's hailing and it's*
                                               snowing.
Il pleut aujourd'hui, il va pleuvoir   *It's raining today, it's going to rain*
   demain et il a plu hier.   *tomorrow and it rained yesterday.*

As in English, there are many idiomatic expressions to describe
the rain, such as **'il pleut des cordes/à verse'** ('it's raining hard/it's
raining cats and dogs').

'LE TEMPS' *TIME*

Le temps is also the French word for *time* – not the precise time
which you read on a watch (this is **l'heure**), but the more abstract
notion of the passage of time or of a length of time.

Je n'ai pas l'heure.   *I haven't got the time. (i.e. I am*
                                               not wearing a watch)

Je n'ai pas le temps de partir   *I haven't got time to go skiing this*
   au ski cette année.   *year.*
Le temps, c'est de l'argent.   *Time is money.*

....
Insight
   In the context of time, **(les) moments** (*moments*, *times*) is a
   useful word:

   Nous avons passé de bons   *We have had/spent good times*
   moments ensemble.   *together.*
....

44a Actuellement, normalement and éventuellement: beware these false friends!

Beware these apparently trustworthy allies! They look friendly enough, but they are classic **faux amis** and have different meanings in French from the English words *actually*, *normally* and *eventually*. You need to be on your guard!

'ACTUELLEMENT' *RIGHT NOW, CURRENTLY*

Elle vit <u>actuellement</u> au Mexique.   *She is living in Mexico at present.*
Elle travaille <u>actuellement</u> dans   *She's working for a publishing*
  une maison d'édition.   *company right now.*

To express the English word *actually*, use **à vrai dire** (*to tell you the truth*) or **en fait** (*in actual fact*). **En effet** (*indeed*) is only used for confirmation:

Ma fille parle bien espagnol mais
  actuellement elle est anglaise. ✗
Ma fille parle bien espagnol mais   *My daughter speaks good*
  <u>en fait</u> elle est anglaise. ✓   *Spanish but in actual fact she*
     is English.

<u>À vrai dire</u>, elle préfère l'espagnol   *Does she actually prefer Spanish*
  au français ?   *to French?*
Oui, <u>en effet</u> !   *Yes, indeed/Yes, that's right!*

'NORMALEMENT'

Normalement is the word used in French when we expect something to happen under normal circumstances or in a normal way:

<u>Normalement</u> elle doit retourner   *We expect her to come back to*
  vivre en Angleterre au bout de   *England to live after three years.*
  trois ans.

| Elle a eu un accident, mais maintenant elle marche <u>normalement</u>. | *She had an accident, but now she is walking <u>normally</u>.* |

When in English we mean *usually*, **normalement, d'habitude** or **généralement** are used:

| <u>D'habitude</u> on va la voir deux fois par an. | *We usually go and see her twice a year .* |

'ÉVENTUELLEMENT'

This is the French word to use when we want to imply that it is possible that something will happen, and not that it will happen in the end:

| <u>Éventuellement</u> elle se mariera avec un Mexicain. | *It is possible that she will get married to a Mexican.* |

Instead, if you wish to indicate that something will happen eventually (i.e. in the end), then **finalement** is a more appropriate word:

Éventuellement elle reviendra chez nous. ✕	
<u>Finalement</u> elle reviendra chez nous. ✓	*<u>Eventually</u> she will come home.*
<u>Éventuellement</u> elle y arrivera.	*<u>One day</u> she may get round to it.*

Used on its own in reply to a question, **éventuellement** means *potentially* or *possibly*.

| **Pourras-tu accepter cela ?** **Oui, <u>éventuellement</u>.** | *Will you be able to get used to that?* *Yes, <u>possibly</u>.* |

44b Some tricky adverbs

'RÉELLEMENT' OR 'VRAIMENT'?

Really!? is often used in English as an exclamation of surprise or disbelief, and it invites the person who has given you a piece of information to confirm it for you. However, **réellement** in French does not convey the same message in French.

Ma fille a maintenant un partenaire mexicain.	*My daughter now has a Mexican partner.*
Réellement ? ✗	
Vraiment ? ✓	*Really?/Is that so?*
Oui, il est vraiment charmant.	*Yes, he's really charming.*

Réellement conveys the more deeply felt *truly* or *honestly*, as in:

Je suis <u>réellement</u> désolé d'apprendre que ta maman est gravement malade.	*I am <u>truly</u> sorry to hear that your mum is seriously ill.*
Cela m'a <u>réellement</u> aidé.	*That was a genuine help.*

'PROPREMENT' *CLEANLY, NEATLY, TIDILY*

Toddlers are encouraged from an early age to **manger proprement**, which means eating without making a mess! If what you mean is the

English *properly*, then consider using phrases such as **correctement**, or **comme il faut** instead. Look at the following examples:

Elle mange proprement – c'est bon
  pour la santé. ✗
Elle mange équilibré – c'est bon   *She has a balanced diet – it's*
  pour la santé. ✓   *good for one's health.*
Il suit les conseils. Il se sert des outils *He's following the advice. He's*
  correctement. ✓   *using the tools properly.*
Je n'arrive pas à le faire comme il faut. ✓ *I'm not managing to do it properly.*

À **proprement parler** means *strictly speaking*, and not 'speaking properly' at it might appear. **Parlez correctement** is what you say to children when you hear them use bad language.

'PRATIQUEMENT' OR 'VIRTUELLEMENT'?

In English we can use the adverbs *practically* and *virtually* to mean 'nearly'. **Pratiquement** is often used in this way in French, but **virtuellement** virtually never!

J'ai virtuellement terminé ce chapitre. ✗
J'ai pratiquement terminé ce chapitre. ✓   *I have nearly finished*
                                               this chapter.

The use of **virtuellement** is more commonly used for descriptions of that which is virtual, i.e. unreal. **Pratiquement** is often used with negative expressions:

Je n'ai pratiquement pas de travail.   *I have almost no work.*
Il n'y a pratiquement personne au   *There is almost no-one in the*
  bureau.   *office.*

Insight

The phrase 'fairly and squarely' survives in French as **carrément** – *straight out* in modern parlance. This is a useful one to master.

Je lui dis carrément ce que   *I tell him straight out what*
  je pense.   *I think*
Vas-y carrément !   *Go for it!*

---

45 Alors, donc, ainsi and aussi

'ALORS', 'DONC' AND 'AINSI'

These three words are interchangeable when what you want to convey is 'for this reason'.

Il pleuvait <u>donc</u> j'ai apporté un parapluie.	*It was raining, so/therefore I brought an umbrella.*
Ils ont perdu le match, <u>ainsi</u> ils sont éliminés de la compétition.	*They lost the match, so they have been eliminated.*
Tu ne veux pas que je t'aide ? <u>Alors</u>, je te laisse.	*You don't want me to help you? In that case, I'll go.*

So can be translated by **si**, but only to accentuate an adjective. Look at this example:

J'étais <u>si</u> content d'avoir ce plan.	*I was <u>so</u> pleased to have this map.*

Otherwise, **si** almost always means *if*:

Si vous avez un plan, apportez-le !	*If you have a map, bring it!*

Stick to **donc**, **alors** and **ainsi** for 'so' in the sense of 'for that reason/therefore':

Je me perds toujours, <u>alors/donc</u> je prends un plan avec moi. ✓	*I keep getting lost, so I take a map with me.*

'ALORS' AND 'DONC' *FOR THAT REASON*

So far, all very straightforward. However **alors** and **donc** both have other more subtle shades of meaning, which you need to find your way around, and which differentiate them from **ainsi**.

Tu te promènes ? Ainsi, moi aussi. ✗

Tu te promènes ? <u>Alors/donc</u>, moi aussi. ✓	*Are you going out for a walk?* <u>*In that case*</u>*, me too/I'll come too.*
Tu ne connais pas le chemin ? Suis-moi donc/Alors suis-moi !	*Don't you know the way? Then/ Well follow me!*
Ce n'est pas par ici, c'est donc par là.	*It's not this way <u>so it must be</u> that way.*

Donc implies that a decision has been made. **Alors** tends to leave the matter undecided, and it is involved in some idiomatic expressions too (e.g. **ça alors !** *well really!*). **Alors** is undoubtedly the most frequently used connecting word in French conversation as it adapts to suit many situations, just like a chameleon! You will often hear people use **alors…** in the same way as we say *well, .. er* in English. See how **alors** is used in the dialogue below.

« <u>Alors</u>…on va au même restaurant que d'habitude ?	*"<u>Well</u>… are we going to the same restaurant as usual?"*
–Eh <u>alors</u> !	*"And why not?"* (a slightly indignant response, here implying 'so what's wrong with that?')
–On essaie un autre <u>alors</u> ?	*"Shall we try another one then?"*
–Ça <u>alors</u> ! »	*"The very idea!"*

Insight

Descartes had been deliberating for a long time before coming to his decisive and philosophical conclusion, '**Je pense donc je suis**' (*I think and therefore I am*).

'AUSSI' *ALSO, TOO, AS WELL*

The most important thing to remember about **aussi** is that you don't start a sentence with it, but put it after the verb.

Aussi j'ai très peu de temps. ✗	
J'ai <u>aussi</u> très peu de temps. ✓	*I also have very little time.*
Moi <u>aussi</u> !	*Me too!*

46 More false friends

FOOD-RELATED FALSE FRIENDS

The following can be amusing:

Il y a beaucoup de préservatifs dans la cuisine anglaise. ✗

Il y a beaucoup de conservateurs/ d'additifs dans la cuisine anglaise. ✓
There are a lot of preservatives/additives in English cooking.

Un préservatif is *a condom*! Imagine telling a Frenchman that you put condoms in your food!

J'achète toujours des produits organiques. ✗

J'achète toujours des produits biologiques. ✓
I always buy organic food.

The adjective **organique** derives from the English scientific definition and describes only the organic matter in soil which derives from plants and animals is not at all the same as the English *organic*. Not very appetising!

Il faut manger des végétaux pour rester en bonne santé. ✗

Il faut manger des légumes pour rester en bonne santé. ✓
To stay healthy you must eat vegetables.

The adjective **végétal** (*vegetable*) is used broadly to refer to the world of living plants. **Les légumes** (*vegetables*) are what we eat.

HEALTH AND BEAUTY

Il est fatigué. Il devrait rester. ✗

Il est fatigué. Il devrait se reposer. ✓
He is tired. He should rest.

Rester has nothing to do with the English *to rest*. It means *to stay*: **Il reste une semaine de plus chez ses parents** (*He is staying one more week at his parents'*); **Pour rester en pleine forme, il fait beaucoup de tennis** (*To stay fit, he plays lots of tennis*).

PLACE PROBLEMS!

J'habite dans une jolie place. ✗	
J'habite dans <u>un</u> joli <u>endroit</u>. ✓	*I live in a nice place.*
<u>Chez toi</u> ou <u>chez moi</u> ?	*Your place or mine?*
Il habite sur la place.	*He lives on the square.*

Une place cannot describe a place to live, but can mean *square* or *seat*:

Excusez-moi madame, c'est ma chaise !	*I'm sorry, but this chair belongs to me!*
Excusez-moi madame, c'est <u>ma place</u> ! ✓	*I am sorry madam, it is my seat!*

Une cité usually means *an estate* or refers to a development of social or subsidised housing; it never means *a city*. Instead, **une grande ville** is used for *city*.

If you want to buy a book, go to **la librairie** (*bookshop*) rather than **la bibliothèque** (*library*) where books will be lent to you, not sold! And if it's wine that you're after, visit the local **cave** (*vineyard shop*) or pop down to your own **cave** (*wine cellar*) for a choice bottle. A visit to the local **caverne** (*cave*) might be rather cold, dark and damp!

Insight

Remember that **terrible** (*terrific, tremendous*) and **formidable** (*great*) are positive adjectives. If you wish to be negative, use **épouvantable** (*terrible, dreadful*) or **horrible**. When describing someone, **sympathique** means *nice* or *likeable*, whereas **compatissant** means *sympathetic* or *compassionate*. If someone is *sensible*, use **sensé** or **raisonnable** to describe them, but use **sensible** for *sensitive*.

Confus is the right word to use for *embarrassed*, but if you are confused **perdu** (*lost*) or **désorienté** (*disoriented, confused*) may be more appropriate. If you have simply not understood something, **Je n'ai pas compris** is the phrase you need.

La vie à Paris est formidable !	*Living in Paris is great!*
Je vous prie de m'excuser, je ne vous ai pas reconnu. Je suis confus(e).	*Please forgive me for not recognizing you. I am embarrassed.*

47 Use dictionaries carefully!

One word in French may be translated many ways in English, and vice versa. So, look beyond the first definition of a word to see whether there are others that might be more appropriate. Most dictionaries give examples showing in which contexts it is appropriate to use a word. Using the wrong translation can cause confusion and embarassment!

A HAIRY BUSINESS!

Je lave mon cheveu. ✗
Je me lave les cheveux.   *I'm washing my hair.*

In the first sentence you are actually saying that you are washing the single hair sticking out of your head! Unlikely to be true! Remember, too, that body hairs for animals and humans are not called **les cheveux** but **les poils**, and that the hair you find in your restaurant soup is **un cheveu**, not **un poil**!

'LE JOURNAL', 'LES NOUVELLES' OR 'LES ACTUALITÉS'?

Every country has its own names for news bulletins and programmes. In France, JT stands for **le journal télévisé**, meaning any televised news programme:

Je regarde le JT de dix-huit heures.   *I watch the six o'clock news.*

The term **les actualités (régionales/nationales/internationales)** refers more generally to regional, national or international news, or current affairs, but not specifically to televised news bulletins. **Le journal**, of course, means *daily newspaper*, and **les actualités régionales** is used for *local newspapers*. **Les nouvelles** is used for more personal news:

Tu as eu de ses nouvelles ?   *Have you heard from him?*
J'ai reçu de bonnes/mauvaises   *I have had good/bad news.*
nouvelles.

'UNE PILE' OR 'UNE BATTERIE'?

Batterie and **pile** both translate as *battery* in English. **Batterie** is typically rechargeable (e.g. for mobile phones, shavers, TV handsets, etc.), whereas **pile** is usually disposable, low voltage (1.5 to 9 volts) and is used in cars.

'UNE BILLE', 'UNE BOULE', 'UNE BALLE' OR 'UN BALLON'?

▶ **Un ballon** is a *balloon* or a *ball* filled with air: e.g. **un ballon de football** (*a football*).
▶ **Une balle** is a small ball, with or without air inside it, usually used for sports, games or hunting: e.g. **une balle de ping-pong** (*a ping-pong ball*), **une balle de tennis** (*a tennis ball*), **une balle de golf** (*a golf ball*) and **une balle de revolver** (*a bullet*).
▶ **Une boule** is solid, not hollow: e.g. bowling, billiard or snooker balls, or even a snowball.
▶ **Une bille** is *a marble*.

'VOLONTAIRE' OR 'BÉNÉVOLE'?

These two words have completely different meanings in French:

Qui est volontaire pour faire la vaisselle ?	*Who is willing to wash the dishes?*
Elle est volontaire pour travailler comme bénévole en Afrique.	*She is willing to work as a volunteer in Africa.*

Un volontaire means *volunteer*, i.e. somebody willing or prepared to do something, regardless of remuneration. **Un bénévole** is an unpaid *voluntary worker*. **Le travail bénévole** is unpaid *voluntary work*.

Insight

It's dangerous to translate idiomatic phrases literally:

Il se jette des fleurs.	*He flatters himself.*
L'argent ? J'aimerais bien en voir la couleur.	*I'd like to see some hard cash.*
Je suis à côté de mes pompes en ce moment.	*I'm not feeling myself at the moment.*
Mettre quelqu'un au pied du mur.	*To call somebody's bluff.*

48 Tu or vous?

Choosing between **tu** (*you*, familiar) or **vous** (*you*, formal and plural) to address a French person needs careful consideration.

To avoid explaining the complex reasons behind the use of **tu** and **vous**, teachers usually simply advise adult students to be cautious and always address another adult using **vous** for all basic verbal exchanges, such as when shopping, stopping someone in the street, or dealing with problems.

Bonjour monsieur l'agent, tu peux m'indiquer où est la gare ? ✗

Bonjour monsieur l'agent, <u>vous pouvez</u> m'indiquer où est la gare ? ✓

Good morning (officer), could you please give me directions to the station?

WHEN TO USE 'TU'

Addressing someone with **tu** indicates that you have a special bond with your interlocutor. This makes its use appropriate when you are talking to:

▶ immediate family members;
▶ close friends;
▶ fellow students of a similar age;
▶ animals.

In general, asking if you can address another person with the word **tu,** as well as whether you may call them by their first name, is normal. Likewise, you should be asked by the other person if you can be addressed as **tu**. Age, rank, social or company position will determine the choice.

Je peux vous tutoyer ?/On se tutoie ?

Can I address you with 'tu'?

Appelez-moi Juliette, je vous en prie !

Please call me Juliette!

WHEN TO USE 'VOUS'

Addressing someone with **vous** is either a mark of respect or the expression of a desire to remain distant and formal. It is normal to use **vous** to address all adults until you get to know them very well, and with people of a more senior position, for people of recognized status (e.g. teachers, priests, managers, police officers) and for strangers.

However, it is not customary to use **vous** when talking to young children, even if they are strangers; they are not used to it and only gain the privilege of being addressed as **vous** when they become adult at eighteen years old. The use of **vous** is, therefore, associated with a symbolic rite of passage between childhood and adulthood.

Using **tu** to address a police officer is not only <u>wrong</u> but can be considered an offence. Whether you are French or not, it could be the start of a regrettable sequence of unpleasant consequences. The same applies to public and private service employees. Using **tu** not only sounds patronizing, condescending and insulting, but will be interpreted as a lack of respect.

Monsieur le directeur, je vous souhaite une bonne journée.	*Have a good day, sir!*
Monsieur Dupont, comment allez-vous ?	*How are you, Mr Dupont?*

Contrast this formal tone with the much more informal:

Pierre, tu vas bien ?	*How are you, Pierre?*
Chéri, ça va ?	*How are you, darling?*

Insight
It is possible to revert from **tu** to **vous** and vice versa. Watching French films, or television, can help you to observe the contexts in which **tu** or **vous** are used.

49 Watch these words!

There are words in every language which need to be used with care. Certain turns of phrase in French have a double entendre, i.e. their meaning may be interpreted in more than one way, which may be suggestive or indelicate. These phrases should be avoided. If, on the other hand, you like to live dangerously try them out and see what happens…!

WHERE SHALL WE MEET?

Une chambre is, without doubt, *a bedroom*. Une pièce mean more generally *a room* in a house and une salle is used for *a room* in a public place. So, if you are attending a conference in a hotel, you need to be wary! Look at the following examples:

On se voit plus tard dans la chambre ?	*Shall we meet up later in the bedroom?*

Grammatically correct, this sentence could, however, bring an unexpected and unwanted visitor to your door! If what you are suggesting is a less intimate meeting, say:

On se voit plus tard dans la salle (de réunion) ?	*Let's meet up later in the (meeting) room.*

'UNE RÉUNION' OR 'UN RENDEZ-VOUS'?

When you attend a business meeting it will be billed as une réunion, but un rendez-vous has social overtones of varying degrees of formality.

Paul a rendez-vous avec Julie ce soir.	*Paul has a date with Julie this evening.*
J'ai (un) rendez-vous chez le dentiste.	*I've got an appointment at the dentist's.*
Je vous donne un rendez-vous avec le docteur Durand.	*I'll give you an appointment with Doctor Durand.*

'MANQUER' *TO MISS*

Manquer needs special attention. To say the following would be very presumptuous:

Je te manque. *You miss me.*

If what you really want to say is that you are missing someone, you need to turn the sentence round:

Tu me manques. *I miss you.*

'UN BAISER' (NOUN) AND 'BAISER' (VERB)

The noun is still in use, but it is probably wiser to use the alternatives **un bisou** or **une bise** (*kiss, peck*) if what you mean is a friendly peck on the cheek. The verb **baiser** is a crude word for sexual intercourse, and is best avoided. Play safe, and if *to kiss* is what you mean, use **embrasser** or **faire la bise**.

Viens ici ! Je vais te baiser avant de partir. ✗

Viens ici que je te fais un gros bisou avant de partir. ✓ *Come here so that I can give you a big kiss before I leave.*

AIMER – *LIKE* IT OR *LOVE* IT?

The fact is that **aimer** can mean either *to like* or *to love*, so it's best to err on the side of caution. Strangely enough, if you use **bien** to qualify the verb, instead of meaning *a lot* it lessens the intensity.

Je t'aime. *I love you.*
Je t'aime bien. *I really like you.*

50 Have fun…but take care choosing between jouir (de), s'amuser, aimer and plaire

At times, whatever the language we are speaking, we all want to express enjoyment and show our appreciation. When it comes to talking about feelings, and to expressing ourselves subtly, choosing the appropriate words is critical. All the above verbs mean *to enjoy* but they are used differently to convey appreciation in different contexts.

'JOUIR'

This is the least versatile of all – and for the most part one to avoid. It has a very limited use in French, suggesting as it does sexual enjoyment and satisfaction. If you want to say more generally that you enjoyed an evening, using jouir is not the way to do it.

J'ai joui hier soir. ✗
J'ai passé une bonne soirée. ✓   *I really enjoyed the evening.*

'Jouir + de'
You can, however, use the verb jouir with de:

La chambre d'hôtel <u>jouit d</u>'une belle vue. ✓   *The bedroom enjoys (i.e. 'benefits from') a beautiful view.*
Il <u>jouit d</u>'une excellente santé.   *He enjoys excellent health.*

'AIMER' AND 'APPRÉCIER'

If you wish to express general pleasure, your best bet is to use the verbs aimer and apprécier. They are versatile and shouldn't get you into hot water!

J'ai joui de ce film. ✗
J'ai beaucoup apprécié ce film. ✓   *I really enjoyed that film.*
Nous aimons faire des promenades.   *We like going for walks.*

'PLAIRE' *TO PLEASE*

Saying *please* is one of the first things you learn: **s'il te plaît** and **s'il vous plaît** quickly become spontaneous. **Plaire** (*to please*) is a useful verb for saying that you like, or enjoy, something, but you need to be careful with the word order and start your phrase with what it is that you like, i.e. the opposite way round from English, as you can see below:

Je te plais ?	*Do you like/fancy <u>me</u>?*
Tu me plais.	*I fancy <u>you</u>.*
La musique nous a plu.	*We enjoyed <u>the music</u>.*
Ce livre lui plaira.	*He will enjoy <u>this book</u>.*

'S'AMUSER' *TO ENJOY ONESELF*

This is the verb to use for just having fun and enjoying yourself. It's a good idea to have one or two phrases prepared in advance so that you can tell other people what a good time you are having.

Je m'amuse bien ici.	*I'm having a good time here.*
On s'amuse bien quand on se voit.	*We enjoy it when we see each other.*
On a passé un bon moment ensemble hier.	*We enjoyed ourselves yesterday.*

Insight

When in doubt, play safe and stick to the verb **aimer** which describes all forms of enjoyment and has no overtones likely to lead to misunderstandings!

'MONTER' *TO ASSEMBLE/GO UP/MOUNT*

Don't be caught out by **monter** whose meaning depends on the context in which it is used:

Pierre, peux-tu m'aider à monter mon meuble IKEA ?	*Pierre, can you help me to assemble my IKEA furniture?*
Peux-tu ensuite le monter à l'étage dans ta chambre ?	*Can you then take it up to your room?*
Tu montes à cheval.	*You ride a horse/You go horseriding.*
Le cheval monte la jument dans le champ.	*The horse mounts the mare in the field.*

Glossary of grammatical terms

Accents Accents are spelling marks above or below certain vowels in French which change their pronunciation or meaning; they include: é, è, ë, à, â, ù, ç.

Adjective An adjective is a word which describes an object or a person, e.g. **silencieux** (*quiet*). There are different types of adjective: demonstrative (*this, that, these, those*); indefinite (e.g. *few, several*); possessive (*my, your, his, her, our, their*).

Adverb An adverb is a word which gives more information about the way an action is carried out, e.g. **silencieusement** (*quietly*).

Article
Definite article: le, la, les (*the*).
Indefinite article: un, une (*a, an*).

Auxiliary verb Avoir or être, used together with a past participle to describe completed actions in the past, e.g. **J'ai quitté Paris** (*I left Paris*), **Je suis allé(e) à Bordeaux** (*I went to Bordeaux*).

Comparative A way of changing an adjective or adverb to compare one with another, e.g. *a bigger car, to drive more speedily*.

Conjunction Words which join two sentences together are called conjunctions, e.g. **et** (*and*), **mais** (*but*).

Consonant Letters of the alphabet with the exception of 'a', 'e', 'i', 'o', 'u' and 'y' in French, are called consonants.

Contraction Contraction occurs when two words are combined by omitting a vowel, e.g. *don't* (*do not*) and in French, **il n'est pas.**

Gerund A noun (in English, ending in -ing) which is derived from a verb, e.g. **parler français, c'est amusant** (*speaking French is fun*).

Gerundive An adjective (in English, ending in -ing) which is derived from a verb, e.g. *the talking clock*.

Imperfect tense The past tense used for descriptions, for activities that used to happen and for interrupted actions, e.g. **La ville était tranquille** (*The town was quiet*), **J'y allais souvent** (*I used to go there often*).

Infinitive The from of the verb given in the dictionary is known as the infinitive, e.g. *to drive*, *to talk*.

Liaison The link made between spoken words to make them easier to pronounce is called a liaison.

Negative The expression of a denial or absence in a sentence, e.g. using **ne...pas** (*not*), **ne...jamais** (*never*), **ne...plus** (*no more*) or **ne... personne** (*nobody*).

Noun A noun is something or someone to which you can give a name, e.g. **table** (*table*), **école** (*school*), **climat** (*climate*). The names we give to people and places, and sometimes to things, are called proper nouns, e.g. Pierre, France, Saturn.

Object The object of a sentence is the person or thing on the receiving end of the action described in the verb, e.g. *I bought a sandwich*.

Past participle The form of a verb (used, in French, with **avoir** or **être**) to speak about completed actions, e.g. **j'ai mangé** (*I have eaten*), **elle est partie** (*she has left*).

Perfect tense/passé composé The tense used to describe completed actions in the past, e.g. **J'ai quitté mon emploi** (*I left my job*).

Plural More than one.

Preposition Prepositions are words such as **à** (*to*), **dans** (*in*), **sur** (*on*) and **entre** (*between*), which indicate the position of something or somebody in relation to another person or thing.

Pronoun Pronouns replace nouns in sentences. Several kinds of pronoun exist in both English and French: 'subject pronouns', e.g. **je** (*I*), **tu** (*you*), **elle** (*she*); 'direct object pronouns', e.g. **me** (*me*), **te** (*you*), **le** (*him, it*); 'indirect object pronouns', e.g. **me** (*to me*), **te** (*to you*), **nous** (*to us*).

These two sentences explain the differences:

1 *I drive John to work. I drive <u>him</u> every day.*

<u>I</u> (subject pronoun) does the action. John is directly on the receiving end of the action, i.e. John is the direct object. <u>Him</u> is a direct object pronoun.

2 '<u>He</u> talks to Mary. He talks <u>to her</u> every evening.'

<u>He</u> (subject pronoun) does the action. 'To her' is an indirect object pronoun.

....

Reflexive (verb) A reflexive verb refers to an action you carry out on yourself, without its involving another person or object, e.g. **se lever** (*to get up*), **s'habiller** (*to get dressed*), **se dépêcher** (*to hurry*). In French an extra word, called a reflexive pronoun (i.e. **me, te, se, nous, vous**) is used to convey this.

....

Stress Stress is the placing of emphasis on one syllable or on part of a phrase.

....

Subject The subject of a sentence is the person or thing doing the action.

....

Superlative A way of changing an adjective or adverb to express the best or worst of its kind, e.g. <u>*the most dangerous*</u>, *she is the one who speaks <u>most quiely</u>*.

....

Syllable A combination of sounds which it is possible to pronounce, usually containing a vowel.

....

Syntax The arrangement of words in a sentence and the way they are connected grammatically.

....

Tense The form of the verb you have to use to show <u>when</u> you do what you do, e.g. *today I am talking* (present tense), *tomorrow I will talk* (future tense), *yesterday I talked* (past tense).

....

Verb An action word which relates what a person does, e.g. **conduire** (*to drive*), **parler** (*to talk*).

Some verbs require a direct object; these verbs are known as transitive verbs, e.g. *to drive a car, to lend a book, to lose a scarf*. Intransitive verbs do not require a direct object, e.g. *to sit, to go, to sneeze*.

....

Vowels The letters of the alphabet 'a', 'e', 'i', 'o', 'u' and, in French, 'y'.

....

In the sentence below you will find examples of some of the terms defined above, followed by an explanation of the grammatical role they play.

John, a quiet man, kindly drove his sister to the hospital and he talked to her to reassure her.

John	proper noun
a	indefinite article
quiet	adjective
man	noun
kindly	adverb
drove	verb (past tense)
his	possessive adjective
sister	noun (direct object)
to	preposition
the	definite article
hospital	noun (indirect object)
and	conjunction
he	subject pronoun
talked	verb (past tense)
to her	indirect object pronoun
to reassure	verb (infinitive)
her.	direct object pronoun

··

Simplified sound system

You may find it helpful to follow this link: www.teachyourself.com
Here you will find a short recording offering guidance on
pronunciation.

Letter(s)	Sound	Approx English sound	French examples
a	'a'	h<u>a</u>t	qu<u>a</u>tre, <u>a</u>mi
ai	'ay'	h<u>ay</u>	l<u>ai</u>t, fr<u>ai</u>s
au(o/eau)	'o'	<u>o</u>ld	ch<u>au</u>d, m<u>au</u>vais
ain/aim/im/in	'ang'	<u>an</u>xious	Bours<u>in</u>, f<u>aim</u>, <u>in</u>téressant, <u>im</u>possible
b	'b'	<u>b</u>aby	<u>b</u>onbons, <u>b</u>ar
c (before a, o, u)	'k' (hard)	<u>c</u>an	<u>c</u>afé, su<u>c</u>re
(before i, e)	's' (soft)	<u>c</u>eiling	<u>c</u>einture, niè<u>c</u>e
ç	's'	fa<u>s</u>t	<u>ç</u>a va, le<u>ç</u>on
ch	'sh'	<u>s</u>ugar	<u>ch</u>apeau, an<u>ch</u>ois
d	'd'	<u>d</u>ad	<u>d</u>ouane, mar<u>d</u>i
e, eu	'uh'	<u>a</u> (indefinite article)	l<u>e</u>, f<u>eu</u>, d<u>eu</u>x
é	'ay'	t<u>a</u>ke	<u>é</u>t<u>é</u>, g<u>é</u>nial
è	'ai(r)'	<u>e</u>rror, <u>e</u>pisode	m<u>è</u>re, p<u>è</u>re
ê, ei	'eh'	p<u>e</u>t	expr<u>è</u>s, t<u>ê</u>te, n<u>ei</u>ge
eau	'oh'	<u>o</u>ld	b<u>eau</u>, l'<u>eau</u>
en	'-ong'	s<u>o</u>ng	d<u>en</u>t, v<u>en</u>t
f	'f'	<u>f</u>at	<u>f</u>évrier, neu<u>f</u>
g	'g' (hard)	<u>g</u>a<u>g</u>	<u>g</u>ants, ba<u>g</u>ue, <u>g</u>uillotine
	'zh' (soft)	ima<u>g</u>e	il <u>g</u>èle, auber<u>g</u>ine, froma<u>g</u>e
h	- (always silent in French)	<u>h</u>our	<u>h</u>iver, <u>h</u>ôpital
i, ï, î, y, in (before vowel)	'ee'	sw<u>ee</u>t	d<u>i</u>x, l<u>i</u>t, <u>î</u>le, <u>i</u>névitable

Letter(s)	Sound	Approx English sound	French examples
j	'zh'	jovial	jambon, déjeuner
k	'k' (rare in French)	keep	kiosque, ski
l	'l'	little	fleurs, mille
m	'm'	mum	madame, comment parfum, embouteillage
n	'n'/'-ng'	noun (nasal vowel)	neuf, noir, un, pain, vin
o	'o'	old	dos, rose
oi	'wa'	chihuahua	boire, trois
ou	'oo'	lose	douze, nous
on	'n'/'-ng'	awning	onze, onéreux
p	'p'	paper	père, soupe
ph	'f'	phone	pharmacie, téléphoner
q	'k'	kick	quinze, banque
r	'r'	- (similar to Spanish 'j', Arabic 'kh')	rouge, ceinture
s	's'	sake	sucre, poisson
sc	'sk'	scold	escargots
	's'	science	scientifique
t	't'	tight	tarte, tomate
th	't'	tea	thé, théâtre
ti (before -on, -ie)	's'	associate	attention, direction, démocratie
u	'u'/'eu'	huge	tu, jupe
ue	'weh'	suede	saluer
ui	'wee'	weed	nuit, fruit
v	'v'	verve	vert, avion
w	'v' or 'w' (in some regional words)	verve	wagon

Numbers in the following Index refer to Chapters 1–50 of this book.

Index to grammar